Praise for

Loving in the Here and Now

"*Loving in the Here and Now* is a rich, comprehensive, and above all, optimistic book. Jane Parsons-Fein demystifies hypnosis. Her clear, explicit instructions, almost like a therapist's physical presence, gently enhance your ability for self-hypnosis and offer a path toward increased self-knowledge and emotional relationship management. Highly recommended."

KITTY LaPERRIERE, PH.D.
Family and couples therapist, and cofounder, American Family Therapist Academy

"A practical guide for couples. With explanations, examples, exercises, and tool kits, Parsons-Fein leads readers to help themselves improve their lives and their relationships."

STEPHEN LANKTON, MSW, DAHB
Author of *The Answer Within: A Clinical Framework of Ericksonian Hypnotherapy*

"A lyrical, deep, and wise book designed to help individuals and couples explore, man, and change the terrain beneath the surface of themselves. An excellent book for therapists as well."

BUNNY S. DUHL, ED.D.
Former co-director, Boston Family Institute

"If you and your partner have drifted apart, here is a guidebook for bridging the distance that has grown between you."

LAWRENCE LeSHANE, PH.D.
Author of *Beyond Technique: Psychotherapy for the 21st Century*

"An excellent, helpful book to assist couples to build—or rebuild—a loving, congruent, joyful relationship."

JOHN BANMEN, PH.D.
Director of Training, Satir Institute of the Pacific

"Parsons-Fein shows us how we work on multiple levels as individuals and couples. Most important, she provides us with a set of pragmatic and emotionally relevant exercises that will help us know our partners and ourselves more intimately. I strongly urge you to explore this book, then open your mind and heart. It will be good for you."

GEORGE GLASER, MSW
Cofounder, Milton H. Erickson Institute of Austin

"Easy-to-follow exercises and engaging examples guide readers to higher levels of understanding and valuable insights. An eminently readable text by a highly respected and revered psychotherapist."

GRAHAM BARNES, PH.D., CGP, FRSA
Author and independent scholar, Inform Lab, Stockholm

"*Loving in the Here and Now* offers thought-provoking ideas about people and the way we relate, and the exercises provide many helpful tactics and suggestions."

ARNOLD A. LAZARUS, PH.D., ABPP
Distinguished Professor Emeritus of Psychology, Rutgers University

"*Loving in the Here and Now* presents valuable insights into recognizing our deadening, latent childhood patterns, together with precious processes for outgrowing their awful limitation on our capacity to love."

JOHN VASCONCELLOS
State Senator of California

"The genius of Jane Parsons-Fein said it simply: 'Understanding your own inner mind's resources for healing can free you to have the relationships you want.' With her years of hard work and dedication to her clients, Parsons-Fein now tells how. If you want to know how to rekindle and develop the relationship you want, this book is a must."

RICHARD LANDIS, PH.D.
Training Director, Southern California Society for Ericksonian
Psychotherapy and Hypnosis

Loving in the Here and Now

JEREMY P. TARCHER / PENGUIN

Loving in the Here and Now

Re-create Your Relationship
and Bring Love
Back into Your Life

Jane Parsons-Fein, CSW, BCD, DAHB

Most Tarcher/Penguin books are available at special quantity discounts for bulk purchase for sales promotions, premiums, fund-raising, and educational needs. Special books or book excerpts also can be created to fit specific needs. For details, write Penguin Group (USA) Inc. Special Markets, 375 Hudson Street, New York, NY 10014.

All names and identifying characteristics have been changed, with the exception of the excerpts and Dr. Ewin.

While the author has made every effort to provide accurate telephone numbers and Internet addresses at the time of publication, neither the publisher nor the author assumes any responsibility for errors or for changes that occur after publication.

Reprinted by permission of the author and publisher. Virginia Satir, the Satir Model, Science and Behavior Books, Inc., Palo Alto, Calif.

Concerning the "River of Life" technique, one may refer to the book *Neugierig aufs Großwerden* by Karl-Ludwig Holtz and Peter Nemetschek. Carl-Auer-Systeme Verlag, 2000.

JEREMY P. TARCHER/PENGUIN
a member of
Penguin Group (USA) Inc.
375 Hudson Street
New York, NY 10014
www.penguin.com

Library of Congress Cataloging-in-Publication Data

Parsons-Fein, Jane.
Loving in the here and now / Jane Parsons-Fein.
p.   cm.
ISBN 1-58542-300-9
1. Man-woman relationships.   2. Interpersonal communication.   I. Title.
HQ801.P37   2004   2003053723
306.7—dc21

Printed in the United States of America
1   3   5   7   9   10   8   6   4   2

This book is printed on acid-free paper. ♾

Book design by Kate Nichols

Author's Note

The experiences in *Loving in the Here and Now* are designed to help you restart and deepen your inner process of emotional healing. On such a journey, all kinds of things can happen. Most surprises are happy ones, but some can lead into unexplored areas of the heart and mind that are difficult and uncomfortable and even troubling. If you find paths that become formidable obstacles, I recommend that you seek guidance from a professional therapist. Some recommendations are found in the appendix at the end of this book. Finding appropriate help can enhance your ability to enjoy your life. It is my hope that this book will inspire, guide, and inform you.

I dedicate this book to you, its readers,

in the hope that my work can help you in

your quest to embrace the truths that heal us

and free us from the delusions

that poison our relationships.

Acknowledgments

For their wit, love of language, and forbearance: My three beautiful sons, Brooks, Tucker, and Nick Parsons.

For the spaciousness of his love and depth of his friendship: Justice Arnold L. Fein.

For being my sister-in-spirit: Kay Thompson, D.D.S., who said, "The dreamer is the true realist."

For the brilliance of their teaching and their inspiring commitment to their art: Milton Erickson, M.D., Virginia Satir, Moshe Feldendkrais, and Bernard Fine, M.D.

For their skillful encouragement: My editor, Denise Silvestro; her assistant, Martha Bushko; and my agents, Jane Dystel and Miriam Goderich.

For their consistent and fun-filled support: Ann and Bruce McCracken, David G. Imber, Mary Knackstedt, Hedi Piel, Rosalie Brody Feder, Frank Don, Ingrid Arenas Lindahl, Sten Lindahl, Gunilla and Anders Lundmark, Ann Wilkens, Solveig Sandstrom-Taylor, Gun Bergstrom, and Leigh Mojica.

For their commitment to growth and love of learning: My colleagues, my students, and my clients.

Contents

THERE IS A WONDERFUL GAME

There is a game we should play,
And it goes like this:

We hold hands and look into each other's eyes
And scan each other's face.

Then I say,
"Now tell me a difference you see between us."

And you might respond,
"Hafiz, your nose is ten times bigger than mine!"

Then I would say,
"Yes, my dear, almost ten times!"

But let's keep playing
Let's go deeper,
Go deeper.
For if we do,
Our spirits will embrace
And interweave.

Our union will be so glorious
That even God
Will not be able to tell us apart.

There is a wonderful game
We should play with everyone
And it goes like this . . .

I Heard God Laughing
Renderings of Hafiz (1320–1389)
By Daniel Ladinsky
Copyright 1996

Preface

Perhaps you came to this book because you've noticed that your relationship has gone stale and you're not sure why. Falling in love was wonderful and now you are not growing in love together. Life seems to have separated you from those early magical moments. Perhaps you and your partner are arguing a great deal or are living in some kind of mutual silence. Disagreements don't necessarily destroy a relationship, but constant fighting can smother romance and push you and your partner further apart until you coexist in icy indifference. Or maybe you have had a series of unsuccessful relationships and are longing for a partnership that is warm, loving, and mutually fulfilling.

This book will teach you how to revitalize an old relationship or jump-start a new one. It will help you create a relationship that is different from the disappointing ones you've had in the past. And it will enable you to communicate with your partner in ways that will draw you closer and create more intimacy. Falling in love was the beginning; growing in love brings even deeper fulfillment.

In my thirty-four years of practice, I have discovered that being able to talk to each other, whether you agree or disagree, is one of the most crucial ingredients of a successful relationship. Oh, I'm sure you've heard it before. You've been told that you have to express your deepest feelings and really listen to what each other has to say, or that men and women come from different planets and you have to understand each other's language. But there are no magic words to say, and the truth is, if you're only listening to each other's words, you're missing the true power of language. You see, it's much more complex than that, and yet it is very simple.

When we speak to each other, we hear the words with our ears, but other parts of us also hear; the words are able to touch the deepest parts of us, parts so well hidden we might not even know they are there. And the messages these words convey have the ability to hurt us, damage us, and cause us to react in ways that seem out of our control.

I first discovered this power of language several years ago. For twelve years I worked in the department of psychiatry at Mount Sinai Hospital. Even with the finely trained staff and the tremendous expenditure of energy and money, I saw minimal improvement in many of our patients, especially after they were discharged and returned home. Many of them were in profound emotional pain. I was frustrated that I couldn't help them more. I felt that something was missing in the way we were working with people.

One Saturday morning I was reading a book in Central Park. Suddenly a paragraph jumped off the page, into my head and into my heart. It described a way of thinking about the human mind and how people relate to each other. It was as if a lightning flash had hit me hard in that one moment. For the first time that I can remember, I made an instant decision with fierce and absolute clarity. I did not care where he was or how long it would take me to find him, I vowed that I was going to learn from this man whose name was Milton H. Erickson, M.D.

The book was *Uncommon Therapy* by Jay Haley. The case written about was of a young suicidal girl. I was struck by how Erickson, a psychiatrist, worked with this girl. She was overweight, had no friends, and felt ugly and unattractive, especially because she had a space between her two front teeth. The only time she brightened up was when she spoke of a young man at work who always appeared at the water cooler when she was drinking water, but never spoke to her. Erickson had someone teach the girl style and grace, help her lose weight and buy new clothes. He also used the hated space between her teeth in an intriguing way. He taught her to become adept at spitting water at a target through the detested space in her mouth. She practiced this until she became very skilled. At Erickson's suggestion she used this skill effectively some time later to attract the young man's attention while at the water cooler by spitting in his face. This got his attention. They are now married.

Erickson gave her something to do by teaching her this trick. He made her use what she hated most about her looks to attract this young man. On an unconscious level, what she had felt as a deficit became the source of a skill she could master to get what she needed for herself. Erickson's way of thinking about how to work with people and their problems was different from anything I had ever been exposed to. His mind was complex, yet it seemed so simple. Erickson believed in the creative healing power in the unconscious part of the mind of each individual. He used language that directed the unconscious to create change.

Freud discovered what he called the "unconscious." Erickson talked with his patients' inner mind, which he also called the "unconscious." Erickson understood the power of the unconscious and how we affect each other with our words, our tone of voice, our bodies. Erickson established an accepting, loving, and guiding relationship with the suicidal girl that she had never had with her parents. Her parents had died and left her a considerable amount of money. Erickson made a deal with her that she could spend all that money on her self-improvement and then decide whether she wanted to kill herself. He clearly communicated his certainty that she would succeed with his verbal and nonverbal language and his gentle and firm acceptance of her. He knew she would succeed and so she did. The girl felt "heard" for the first time in her life, and she learned to be playful.

Erickson believed that we all move in and out of automatic consciousness, which he called hypnotic trance. We shift from one state of awareness to another all the time. You can be sitting at your desk paying bills and you hear a piece of music that shifts you into a reverie. You sit back, close your eyes, and go somewhere far away. This shift can also be caused by people's voices or by what they say. When we are in this receptive state we take in stimuli and information on deeper and richer levels. Our bodies are as affected as our minds. For example, you can be struggling to solve what seems to be an insoluble problem; you just give up and go into a daydream and all of a sudden the solution becomes clear to you. In a hypnotic trance, people can hear suggestions and then discover their own ways of achieving what they want. Emile Coué, a nineteenth-century French pharmacist, is famous for his self-hypnotic statement: "Every day, and in every way, I am becoming better and better." His definition of hypnosis was "the ability to use suggestion."

Understanding your own inner mind's resources for healing can free you to have the relationships you want. Do you know that a part of your inner mind is trying to protect you? It has attempted to keep you safe from the time you were very little. This part of our mind is focused on survival and always thinks in the concrete ways we thought as children. It has no sense of time or space. It responds to action words. For example, when you say to a child, "Now don't spill the milk!" the child will probably spill the milk because the action verb, "spill," is stronger than the negative command.

This inner mind operates when our feelings run deep and we perceive danger to our sense of security. That is why the perception of rejection or abandonment causes us to do or say things that are not quite rational. We can become aware of how this primitive, always-on-the-alert survival mind operates in our relationships, and then we can change our responses.

Many of us fear abandonment by a loved one. This may go back to the infant's terror when the mother leaves and he feels separate and alone. Many people hold on to painful relationships because the terror of separation is felt by this survival part of the mind as abandonment and death. People often withhold their feelings because of this fear of loss, and the relationship suffers. Most of us are not aware of this deep-seated fear, but it can destroy our relationships and dictate our lives.

Sometimes, when you react automatically, seemingly without thinking, or say or do something you later regret, this part of your mind has reacted. It is doing its best to protect you. Perhaps you got so angry at your partner that you stopped talking to him for several days. You pouted. You retreated into silence. Part of you was trying to protect you. The problem is, this behavior doesn't work. It usually only makes matters worse. If it happens over the years it can chill a relationship into an iceberg. What was warm becomes cold; what was important goes underground or, sadly, disappears altogether.

When you become attuned to what this protective part of you is doing and invite it to align with your whole self, you can change your behavior and your relationship. When a client walks into my office, he or she brings along a whole lifetime of memories, thoughts, feelings, learnings, and disappointments that are conscious and unconscious, recognized and invisible. My job is to offer that client tools to discover his or her own unconscious and to develop the unique ability to create a life that is more joyful and serene, rather than a life that is in bondage to the survival fears of childhood.

So how can you come to terms with this mysterious part of yourself? You can become familiar with it by practicing the self-observation that you can learn in this book. Practice can help you just as practice taught you how to read. You can discover how you choreographed your life to protect your sensitive inner self, and perhaps to push people away. You can learn how your unique mind sets up its own ways to protect you—ways that may have worked when you were little but are now counterproductive—and you can harness its creativity to expand, rather than to limit, your experience.

Your inner mind is a powerful, creative energy and you can learn to use it to redesign your relationships. You can learn to design your life by generating your choices instead of reacting to what life brings you. You fell in love. Now you can grow in love.

We all develop defense mechanisms to deal with what may be too painful to confront head-on. This is part of growing up, of adapting to our unique personal environment. A little boy's father may be infuriated that his son won't share his truck with his little sister and spank him. If these spankings become a pattern, the little boy may repress his anger, deny his own needs, and let his sister have his toys. The inner part of his mind is defending himself from feeling his father's disapproval. Later, he may "accommodate" his wife and let his wife take whatever she wants. A little girl who has been sexually abused and sworn to secrecy by the perpetrator will become secretive and untrusting in many ways that can affect her relationships, even as an adult.

Following is an example of how this part of our mind can create solutions that do not work. In this case it is physical: a headache that lasted for twenty-five years.

This is a true story of a man we will call Abraham Curtis. For almost twenty-five years he suffered from persistent headaches. He went from one clinic and doctor to another, but no one could find a physiological cause for his pain. One day he went to a doctor in New Orleans who, after thoroughly questioning Abraham, learned that the headache had started after a jeep accident during the war in Israel. Abraham awoke in the military medical station with the headache, which never went away. It is unclear whether he was discharged because of the headache.

The doctor, Dabney Ewin, a surgeon who does medical hypnosis, did a hypnotic induction and Abraham went into trance, an altered state of consciousness in which he was able to relax his conscious mind so that his unconscious mind could accept suggestions and make use of them. Dr. Ewin said to Abraham's inner mind, "The war is over." Abraham awakened and, because the survival part of his mind understood the suggestion, the headache was gone, never to return. Abraham later said in a moment of personal insight that he thought his unconscious had learned that he no longer needed the pain to keep him from returning to combat.

There are many examples of how this part of our mind works overtime to ensure our survival. And because we are all unique, there are an infinite number of creative mechanisms that people's minds invent.

Take Amy, an accountant and the mother of three. She went into the hospital for a surgery that was successful, but after the surgery the pain did not go away. The doctors had no answers. She had to take care of her three little children but could barely get out of bed. Someone suggested hypnosis since nothing else had helped.

In hypnosis, she reviewed what she had felt and thought during the surgery. She suddenly remembered that at one moment she became terrified that she was dying. Then she remembered feeling the pain in the recovery room and being so grateful that she was alive. "That pain in my back meant that I was alive!" she said. In trance she was told that she could feel comfortable *and* stay alive. Her unconscious accepted the suggestion. The pain disappeared for good and she went home fully confident that she could manage.

Jennifer was a lively, funny, wholesome young designer who spent many years and underwent exhaustive testing trying to get pregnant. The tests came up with no answers. Jennifer and her husband, Tom, were in excellent health. After much heartache and frustration, they began to consider in vitro fertilization. Jennifer and I decided to try hypnosis, just in case some experience she had forgotten was creating the obstacle. Jennifer came upon a memory of when she was two years old. She watched her mother collapse in grief upon hearing that her sister had died in childbirth. In trance, Jennifer said, "If I have a baby I'll die, too, just like Auntie Jean, and my mother will go to bed and not get up!" Jennifer and I worked together to tell this little-girl protective part of her mind that she could safely have her baby. She became pregnant soon afterward and delivered a beautiful baby boy. Jennifer now has four children.

Each of these cases is an example of how, in a moment of emotional upset, the reasoning part of the mind gets suspended and the inner part of our mind comes to the fore and makes decisions designed to protect us. During these moments, this hyperalert inner mind can take in the trauma and make decisions that affect us profoundly long after we have forgotten the upsetting event. This part of our mind is not affected by time or reality. Jennifer could look around and see that many mothers lived through childbirth, but her little-girl mind that was frozen with fear could not see around her, just as the traumatized part of Abraham's mind held on to the headache in spite of the passage of time.

While each of these people reacted physically to upsetting experiences, some people react emotionally with behaviors that affect their relationships. Instead of a twenty-five-year headache, or postsurgical pain, or an inability to conceive a child, these survival learnings manifest themselves when we lash out at our partner and overreact, or when we shut down, withdraw, and pull away, or when we replay the same painful pattern in different relationships.

The nervous system of every child is sensitive to outside stimuli. That is how we learn consciously and unconsciously. A child can spend years sitting quietly and rigid at the family dinner table because the family rule is that children are to be seen and not heard. Even as an adult, sitting at the family dinner table can produce the exact same helpless feelings. Or a child who witnessed years of tension and arguments at the family dinner table can develop indigestion at holiday times when the family comes together. Words and phrases, as well as tones of voice or facial expressions, can evoke the painful childhood responses in adults, often outside of their awareness.

When some automatic reaction or pattern overtakes you, is this a clue that your inner mind is involved, reenacting its need to protect you from the pain or the danger of earlier, long-forgotten experiences? Think about it. When you suddenly get angry at your partner for no obvious reason, are you blaming your partner because you don't yet understand the true source of your painful reactions? Do you often get irritated by some characteristic in your partner and have no clue as to why? You can learn how to explore this irritation and you may come up with a surprising answer. When you pinpoint the wound, the irritation will disappear.

The first time James and Gina walked into my office they were barely speaking. As often happens, each wanted me to "fix" the other. James said Gina complained about everything, while Gina asserted that her husband would just shut down and give her the silent treatment whenever they disagreed. Their one-sided arguments ranged from whether to get tuna canned in oil or water to whether to go to the ocean or the mountains on vacation. Gina would say what she wanted and if James had a different opinion he would become silent and stiff. When we explored their family backgrounds using genograms (described in chapter three), we discovered that Gina had been told, "If you love me you'll tell me what is bothering you, even if it hurts my feelings." James was constantly told, "If you can't say something nice, don't say anything at all." Gina perceived James's silence as an absence of love. He thought he was being loving by not saying anything, doing it her way, although resenting it deep down inside. Both had been programmed to respond to disagreements in different ways. Their different styles of relating—styles that were ingrained in them early on—were causing them problems. As we worked together, James realized he had to teach himself how to shift out of his withholding pattern, and Gina learned that his tight-lipped silence did not mean he didn't love her, so she could relax.

Susie and Willy had sexual problems that had escalated to the point where they decided they needed counseling or else they would likely divorce. Doing their genograms, we discovered that Susie had constantly been told, "Boys will always take advantage of you!" Willy remembered the refrain: "Women like strong men!" Willy would try to assert his needs forcefully, which drove Susie further and further away, and this in turn made Willy more anxious and therefore more assertive. These unrecognized patterns were contributing to the breakdown of their relationship in every area. Like most of us, neither Susie nor Willy recognized the difference in their family programming about sexuality and gender and what it was doing to them. They just knew they were unhappy.

We all have these unspoken problems that go on in relationships. We all have "hot buttons" that get pushed by a word, phrase, facial expression, an anniversary date, a sudden memory. We often respond automatically. Something comes in from left field that sends us into fury, deep silence, or total confusion.

To have successful relationships we need to do several things:

* recognize our own automatic responses and shift out of them;

- shortcut these responses so that we react to the "now" instead of to past hurts;
- recognize our partner's "buttons";
- learn how to respond when he/she is operating on automatic rather than reacting to the moment.

LOVING IN THE HERE AND NOW is about halting the downward spiral of your relationship by helping you do detective work with your inner mind, giving you the tools to build a creative relationship and be surprised and delighted at what your own awarenesses can reveal. You will find many case examples that show how our powerful inner minds affect our everyday emotional life and what we can do about it. You can learn about your unique history and use the exercises at the end of each chapter to help you develop a working relationship with this powerful, creative part of yourself.

Awareness is your main tool. By practicing the exercises in this book you can learn how to make distinctions in your feelings and to become attuned to how you shift from one state of consciousness to another. By pinpointing where your emotional feelings are located in your body, you can learn to track them before they amplify out of control. Thus you can use your internal states as a barometer for the expression of your feelings, thoughts, hopes, wishes, and dreams. Most important, you can develop a trusting relationship with your own inner self, which will open up new avenues for knowing how and when to trust others.

The chapters are arranged in sequence to help you build your self-awareness and your knowledge of your own unconscious one stage at a time. The beginning chapters lay the groundwork and we work toward the important areas of money and sexuality, which plague so many of us. Later chapters will be more helpful to you if you do the preliminary work with the earlier chapters to develop the tools you will need later. Consistent practice will make them easier and richer.

The adventure of learning more about yourself can bring you closer to your partner.

Working with the inner mind goes back to ancient times. The laying on of hands is a form of hypnosis in the Bible. In the eighteenth century, Anton Mesmer, an Austrian physician, practiced what he called "animal magnetism," which was based on his belief that a mysterious fluid penetrates all bodies and allows one person to have a powerful "magnetic" influence over another.

Contrary to popular opinion, therapeutic hypnotism is not black magic; it does not force people to do things unconsciously that they would not do consciously. But studies have shown that anything you can do consciously, you can do better when you are in a trance state.

There are various forms of hypnosis: medical hypnosis, which can help people control pain and heal more effectively; clinical hypnosis, which can help people develop self-esteem, overcome performance anxiety, discover unremembered events, and use new ways of creativity; stage hypnosis, in which suggestible people can perform acts to entertain audiences; laboratory hypnosis, which is used for research; sports hypnosis, to help athletes develop their coordination and endurance; and theater hypnosis, which can help performers work with anxiety and enhance their creativity. Hypnosis can be induced by yourself or by an outside stimulus or person, or it can be spontaneous. All hypnosis is self-hypnosis because you use your own ability to shift into trance and use the suggestions you receive. An example of spontaneous trance is when you hear a piece of music and lose all track of time. You bring your own unconscious associations to the words, the music, the symphony. A sudden shock or surprise also shifts us into an automatic response in which we disconnect from the moment and go inward. Moving into trance is a natural experience we all have, and when we become more aware of slipping into it, whether it is positive or negative, we can use it with effectiveness and pleasure.

Freud discovered the unconscious and laid the groundwork for the idea that we each have a part of our mind that works in mysterious ways. Milton Erickson, said to be the greatest medical hypnotist in our time, demystified hypnosis and developed effective ways of talking to and with the unconscious.

LOVING IN THE HERE AND NOW is founded on the work of Milton Erickson; Virginia Satir, a pioneer family therapist; Moshe Feldenkrais, an Israeli physicist who did hypnosis with the body that he called "Awareness Through Movement"; and Kay Thompson, D.D.S., an artist of hypnotic language. This book interweaves their approaches so that you can learn to apply these groundbreaking techniques to your own life.

Discovering my own inner mind with the help of these pioneers and many others has been one of the great adventures of my life. Hopefully it will become one of the great adventures of yours.

Introduction

This is a book about love—that most essential and dramatic of human experiences. When two people fall in love, their hearts open to each other with innocence, tenderness, playfulness, and passion. The world seems transformed and everything seems magical. With this loving openness comes a great vulnerability as well.

Our first experience of loving intimacy came when we were infants. The deep bonding of parent and child is reactivated when we fall in love; our unfulfilled childhood longings can also be reactivated. Our deepest feelings come into consciousness, which is why we experience the heightened sensitivity that is part and parcel of intimacy. There are also the more painful experiences of having our old wounds and unmet needs so close to the surface that they are easily activated by those we love. But having our hurts so available is an incredible opportunity to heal them if we know how. Learning how is the purpose of this book. Falling in love becomes growing in love.

Naomi came to me because she and her new husband, Richard, were having marital problems. Naomi and Richard got married after a short and passionate courtship. Naomi, thirty-seven, had been a set designer and had given up a successful career when she got married because she wanted to decorate and set up a beautiful home and have a baby soon. Richard, forty-two, was a divorced lawyer with no children. The two embarked on their marriage with great expectations because they were deeply attracted to each other and shared many interests.

Shortly into the marriage Naomi began to feel insecure and unsettled. Richard complained that she was too controlling and overbearing. Matters reached a peak the first time Richard went on a business trip and didn't call when he had said he would. It was like a knife through Naomi's heart. How could he? Her intense reaction came from a place she didn't understand, and though she knew there might be some explanation for his not calling on time, she didn't answer the phone for two days! Crazy behavior? Perhaps. But most of us are capable of these kinds of reactions when our expectations of a loved one have been frustrated.

Concerned about her response, Naomi set up an appointment with me. A week later, when she arrived late for our appointment, she was still fuming. She started right in blaming Richard. After all, he had told her exactly when he would call and he didn't telephone. "Wasn't that inconsiderate of him?" she asked me. I gently suggested that perhaps his flight had been delayed or maybe the meeting had run longer than expected. I then asked her if she was curious about the intensity of her reaction. She admitted that there might have been a valid reason for his not calling, and maybe she had overreacted, but she just couldn't control the panic she felt. She had gone on automatic and had just stopped talking to him.

Using hypnosis, I helped her relax and explore similar times in the past when she had had such feelings. She went into a hypnotic trance and remembered how frightened she had felt when her father went away for long periods of time; her mother became depressed and angry and little Naomi felt helpless. Through hypnosis, she recognized the roots of her fear of abandonment that she had relegated to the back of her mind. Although Naomi knew consciously that her father had spent most of her childhood on long business trips, she was unable to make the connection with her new husband's first business trip and the panic she felt. As Erickson said, "The easiest things to see are often overlooked."

Naomi had blocked out her earliest fear of abandonment—her father's leaving for extended periods of time—beause it was too painful for her to face as a child. But this fear recurred in Naomi's adult life. The fear was hidden, but it influenced her nevertheless. Once I pointed out the possible connection between Naomi's childhood fear and her adult behavior, she could then explore the root of her fear and begin to take control of it. She soon came to see that the intensity of her love for Richard had brought all these feelings to the surface again. Because she was committed to Richard and to making their relationship work, Naomi learned to deal with her discomfort.

This is also a book about the inner mind. Understanding this inner part of ourselves is the key to discovering the sources of those painful, recurring hurts and destructive ways of relating that can erode the experience of love between you and your partner. These painful patterns are not "just the way I am" or "just the way my partner is." They come from somewhere. They were learned at some point. By understanding how your inner mind learns, you can see these relationship problems with new eyes, expand your knowledge of yourself, and develop greater compassion for yourself and your partner, just as Naomi did. Together with your partner, you can discover that there are hidden resources of healing and creativity available to you both. (You can also discover this by yourself if your partner is unwilling to work on this with you, or if you don't have a partner.)

Lastly, this is a book about the special state of consciousness called trance. When you are in trance you can become more clear about how your inner mind learns and how it heals. LOVING IN THE HERE AND NOW teaches you to recognize the everyday trance states that you experience all the time without realizing it. It teaches you about the negative trances that couples in pain so often evoke in each other. Most important, it teaches about positive trance, the state we can use not only to understand, heal, and shift out of these negative patterns and states, but also to enhance the experience of connection, intimacy, and even physical pleasure in our relationships.

Understanding trance can also sensitize you to language, to the way you talk to yourself and the way you talk to your partner. Our language shapes our reality and our relationships. "You don't really love me!" is not just a statement made in pain and anger. It can become a strong suggestion if heard at a particularly vulnerable moment and/or is repeated enough. "You always interrupt me!" or "You never listen to me!" can be heard by the unconscious as a suggestion that your partner may take on as an automatic trance behavior. An unhappy husband said to me, "She has told me so many times that I don't love her that I find myself feeling love less and less and feeling anger more and more."

Becoming aware of how we talk to ourselves is the first step toward mastering our reality. We can begin to see that how we talk to ourselves affects how we talk to our partners and in fact shapes our entire lives. There are dialogues that go on all the time inside our minds but outside of our awareness. Often they are in the form of judgments and criticisms, and although we may not be conscious of these messages, they affect us profoundly. They influence our perceptions and what we say, how we say it, and how we behave in response to these perceptions. In turn, our behaviors influence our partners' actions.

When Naomi did not receive the promised phone call, her mother's voice began, "If he loved me enough, he wouldn't go away all the time!" "I wonder if he is with that other woman." "Is he going to leave me?" Naomi began to take on the same behavior that she had seen in her mother. She became critical, overbearing, even whining. This was her automatic response to the subliminal messages she was getting from her own inner survival mind. She was beginning to set up an unhappy marriage—similar to the marriage of her parents—without consciously recognizing what she was doing.

Habitual language is familiar and easier and often keeps us stuck in old unwanted places. Couples can discover together the source of this language—the unmet needs and unhealed wounds from their child-hoods—and then learn to short-circuit these automatic responses.

Just as our negative self-talk can evoke negative responses in our partners, our accepting self-dialogue can bring about a positive reaction in our partners when it is communicated truthfully. Naomi shared with Richard the painful feelings she had, the helplessness she felt when she heard her mother's constant haranguing of her father, and her terror that she was beginning to behave the same way. Richard was touched, took her in his arms, and no longer felt resentful. They moved through that dark place together and came out stronger as a team.

Couples can learn the specific ways in which they unconsciously use words and body language to disenchant each other. They can learn to turn automatic responses into accepting, flowing, and naturally spontaneous communication. They can also become aware of the power of language to enhance and heal their relationship.

How Hypnosis Can Transform Your Relationship

Sally entered therapy because she was in a seven-year marriage that she had tried to terminate three times, only to reunite with Don each time. Neither she nor Don had been able to commit to the other, yet they were unable to split up. A recent session proved to be a turning point for them, powerfully revealing that their current problems were deeply rooted in their original family behavioral patterns.

In this important session Don, red-faced, eyes bulging, leered menacingly in Sally's face and told her how he hated her. Sally had turned pale and wide-eyed as Don's voice became louder and louder until he was yelling at her, two inches from her face. Her breathing became short and she didn't move a muscle. She just stared blankly at him. I knew she had moved into a self-absorbed state that I call a negative trance. I also knew that Don was losing control. I intervened. My question was designed to help her find the source of her pain. I had taught her self-hypnosis so she was able to recognize when she shifted into a spontaneous trance.

"Sally, how old do you feel right now?" I asked. Don slumped back into his chair. Sally answered my question in a monotone. She described the following scene: "I am four years old and Father is strapping the boxing gloves on me. I know that he is expecting me to let my little brother box with me until I start to cry. Then Father will stop the match. I want to please Father so I always let Seth win." This was the first time in our work together that Sally remembered this oft-repeated scene. Don's shouting had triggered Sally's whole body into reliving the shock and pain of her experience as a four-year-old. Now she was sobbing and Don sat red-faced, staring at her coldly. There was a long silence.

Then she blinked, took a deep breath, and looked at me. "Getting beaten up by Seth was the way I could please my father! My God! I have been repeating that all these years! It's the story of my life!" Color came back into her face. This revelation was a profound shift in her therapeutic work.

In her adult life Sally had been married three times, twice to alcoholics, once to a batterer. During her seven-year relationship with Don, she had attempted to leave repeatedly, but somehow was always

compelled to go back to him. His explosiveness hurt her and sometimes made her feel ill, but she just couldn't leave him.

After this session, Sally finally understood the unconscious survival behavior she had repeated in all her intimate relationships with
men. In effect, as a child she had been hypnotically programmed into
a pattern that had been imprinted so deeply that she forgot it. The
newly remembered boxing scene became symbolic to her of the many
times she had negated her own feelings to please her father. In addition, by doing her family genogram, a model I will explain in chapter
three, she came to understand that her father had been brought up
to ignore *his* feelings and had unconsciously passed his self-denial on
to her.

When Don yelled at her, she shifted into the negative little-girl
state that had kept her stuck. In therapeutic hypnosis she learned to
recognize this shift in her feelings and to step back and shift back to
her adult self. This is the essence of the therapeutic trance—being in
the experience and watching it at the same time. With practice she began to see her father with new eyes and to separate him from Don.

Sally and I worked with self-hypnosis until she was able to recognize quickly when she moved into her little-girl trance and to shift out
of it. She was meeting many parts of herself that she hadn't yet experienced. She learned that she had the right to say no when something
didn't suit her, to stand up for herself and not accept toxic behavior
from her partner. As a child she had learned the style of thinking and
the language of the placater, but now she was learning how to shift out
of that mind-set and stand on her own two feet.

But this story is not about Sally's being stuck in an abusive relationship. It is about two people being stuck in an abusive relationship.
As the old saying goes, it takes two to tango. Don was also stuck in his
own negative trance. When Don was a small child his father disappeared, leaving him to be reared by three generations of cold and
withholding women who fought constantly with each other. He never

experienced the nurturing he needed, and as a little boy he learned that the only way to communicate was to blame someone else. It was the only language he knew. Sally's own withholding behavior inflamed his rage. It reminded him of the women who had raised him. The angrier he became the more she drew away, and the more she withdrew the angrier he became. They held each other in a reflexive loop that was automatic and uncontrollable. This could be described as a negative hypnotic trance that came from the early programming in each of their families. Each reinforced in the other the deprived feelings they had experienced as children.

I taught Don self-hypnosis and he went back to the tumultuous scenes with his mother, aunt, and grandmother. He came upon many painful memories that he had repressed long ago. When he realized how confused and frightened that little boy had been, he saw his own experience from a new perspective and wept for the little helpless boy who had no place to run to. He also saw how he repeated those scenes from his childhood in his adult life.

Don learned to recognize the triggers in his own mind that set off his rage, to step back and remind himself that he was now an adult and no longer helpless. With practice he learned how to shift out of that helpless state before his anger escalated. Using many memories of his own childhood experience, Don got in touch with the fear that was at the root of his anger. Don was able to learn compassion for the little boy he used to be, and therefore for Sally, and he eventually could communicate his anger without leering into her face. He had integrated that little boy into his own big and aching heart.

Sally and Don were able to bypass their automatic responses and connect with and respect their own and each other's vulnerability. Seeing the human vulnerability in each other, they rediscovered what had attracted them to each other in the first place. They found that their basic respect and love for each other was strong enough to form a foundation for new patterns they could create together.

Once Don and Sally recognized that the painful states they evoked in each other actually had their roots in their respective family histories, the tendency to blame each other decreased. Through self-hypnosis, they learned to shift out of these states when they felt them emerging. These moments don't disappear, but they are seen for what they are and managed differently—with a little more distance and greater compassion.

Perhaps the most important thing I teach in this book is learning how to shift out of these negative relationship trances, because this is the key to stopping the downward spiral of a relationship. People who watched their parents fight, scream at each other, get violent, or refuse to speak to each other and who therefore lived in a state of tension have a profound impact on their own children. As we have said, the imprints can go underground, only to show up later when the infant or child has grown up. Tracking these imprints, pinpointing the feeling before it escalates, and shifting out of that trance state can bring miracles to your relationship when you are willing to cope with those internal and unwanted demons. Those demons were in the minds of your parents, possibly your grandparents. They go from one generation to another underground, and it is important for the next generation to take charge of them. This is the hard work and well worth it. There *is* a light at the end of the tunnel.

These lessons will work for you when both you and your partner do them even when the going gets tough, because that is usually when you make the most progress. By working through your discomfort you can achieve great breakthroughs in the understanding of yourself and of your partner. These exercises can also result in a newfound energy and playfulness in your relationship. When you make the commitment to this process, you give your relationship the chance to grow deeper and stronger.

Doing the exercises in this book may give you a doorway to new perspectives on how you can work with each other. If your partner refuses to partake in these exercises, you can do them yourself and you can still have a good impact on your relationship. By recognizing your negative trances and learning how to shift out of them, you will change your behavior and this, in turn, will affect your partner's behavior, whether it is a present partner or a future partner.

The Adventure Begins

Throughout this book I will guide you through the process in which you become more self-aware and can uncover the unconscious messages that affect your relationship. The first chapter describes hypnosis and trance. You will learn how you shift from one state of trance to another and how you can recognize these changes of consciousness that you may never have noticed. When we move into these vulnerable states within our inner minds we all are more receptive to suggestion, whether the suggestions are negative or positive. You will become more familiar with what hypnosis is and why it is your best tool for change. You will learn how to use it every day to help yourself.

Have you ever wondered why you keep repeating the same behavior although it never works? In chapter two you will learn about the power of imprinting, which is how your unconscious mind reacts when you are in trance. You store imprinted memories in a way that differs from experiences your conscious mind is monitoring. You will learn what imprinted you in your own original family. More important, you will learn how to recognize when you are reliving your family consciousness. I call this the family trance and everybody has one.

In chapter three you will learn more about family trance and how it affects people's lives. You will also learn how you move into your own family trance. You will do your own detective work and discover the family programming you may not have known you had. You will learn how to track and trace your own family history, your family consciousness, and your family-endorsed codes of behavior. You will see how your family's attitudes, secrets, and myths can have a profound effect on your life.

Your family genogram and questionnaire will help you pinpoint the invisible family patterns that have influenced your life choices. By doing the genogram, you can trace events in the experiences of the people who lived several generations before you were born and see how historical events and their relationships with each other shaped them. People who were just names to you can come alive and you may discover how what they did and said is still affecting your life.

In chapter four you will discover the emotional survival tools you developed in your childhood and the triggers that reactivate them in the present. You will also learn how to recognize and disempower the anchors and anniversaries that hold you emotional hostage to the past. You will learn to recognize your own emotional blind spots.

In chapter five you will learn to tune in to your inaudible self-talk that influences your attitudes and choices. You will discover where your self-criticism comes from and how it brings you down. You probably never paid much conscious attention to the elusive ways parts of yourself talk to you. Often they are the inner voices you have absorbed from your family. You will recognize strengths you didn't know you had. Warm and beautiful memories woven into your life can come into relief when seen against the multigenerational tapestry of your very own family history. The invisible chains of parenting become visible so that you can free your relationship from them, keeping the strengths and letting go of the rest.

In chapter six you will become familiar with the conscious and unconscious parts of yourself. We are constantly shifting consciousness from one part to another, often unaware of the changes. Virginia Satir developed a model that she called "the Iceberg." The top of the iceberg, which is our behavior, is expressed at the conscious level. Under the surface are expressions of the unconscious parts of ourselves that often developed at certain critical times in our lives. Moving to the deeper levels of feeling that accompany these parts can help you to gain control as you shift from conscious to unconscious responses and to recognize that you are more than the sum of your parts.

Chapter seven will help you become more exquisitely aware of the parts of yourself that you may have split off or denied, or that you don't want to look at. They may be ugly, or nerdy, or helplessly boring. You may harbor feelings of shame about them. It is as if they are sitting in the back of your mind in some dark place, feeling sorry for themselves or waiting to be rescued. Many people are surprised and delighted at what they find, especially as they become more attuned to their own unconscious. Becoming aware, they discover compassion for these parts of themselves and a new dimension in their inner lives, which brings them more fully into the present moment.

Chapter eight focuses on how to convert the power of anger into creative energy in your relationship before it wreaks havoc. Anger is energy and does not disappear just because you repress or suppress it. Unexpressed anger comes out in crooked ways. You may be fighting the wrong battle.

Chapter nine brings money myths to the surface, where you can deal with them. The most devastating disagreements that couples can have are about money and sex. Deep-seated and chronic, they have been imprinted onto the couple's psyches, keeping them locked into overt battles and covert disagreements. You can learn how to cope with the differences of opinion that can be irrational and primitive. You can go beyond the boundaries of your programmed thinking and feeling by doing the exercises in this chapter.

Chapter ten focuses on the big one—sexuality, which is the ultimate trance state. You will learn how to use your ability to let yourself go into trance to promote emotional and sexual intimacy. Partners can learn to become more deeply relaxed and spontaneous with each other by practicing playfulness, self-suggestions, and new behaviors to enhance physical experience.

Most important, you can develop nonjudgmental self-observation and let go of self-criticism. Self-criticism, conscious and/or unconscious, can play havoc with sexual and sensuous pleasure and emotional closeness. We are all hypersensitive to our own and our partner's sexual performance. Feelings run deep and can go underground to emerge as a toxic influence in many other areas. The exercises in this chapter will help you explore your unique humor, playfulness, and creativity as doorways into closeness and deep connection.

Chapter eleven is a summary of how we have been working with your unconscious and a review of all that you have done. It focuses on your body and the messages it sends your inner mind. Becoming aware of your body and how it moves and shifts as you go from one state of consciousness to another is a major theme of this book. We will look at all you have worked with and also at the obstacles that may have come up or will come up as you continue to learn about yourself and your partner. You can practice teaching your body to listen to your mind and your mind to listen to your body.

Working out in the gym is not enough to sensitize you to your body. Every feeling you have is preceded by subtle physical changes. By tuning in to your body you can track your physical and emotional changes and enjoy them. Couples have profound physical effects on each other. By learning how to listen to your body, you can coach each other in ways that can enhance your physical well-being. This certainly is preferable to giving each other a headache, stomachache, or shattered nerves.

Chapter twelve will put together what you have learned and changed and what you still want to work with. We will look toward the future. As each of you comes closer to yourself, you can come closer to each other. Falling in love becomes growing in love.

There is an exercise for a monthly review of your relationship and information on how you can continue to expand your awareness of yourself and your partner. You can pinpoint the changes in your behavior and your partner's behavior that you have noticed or can now pay attention to. You can even begin to enjoy your disagreements when each of you is true to your own feelings. As we all know, progress is two steps forward and one step backward, so this chapter will also address what to do when you backslide so that you can continue to move forward.

The exercises are not difficult, but they may bring up memories, feelings, or revelations that may make you uncomfortable for the moment. But keep in mind that you are uncovering these things so that you can control them and move past them.

The biggest challenge will be for you to make the time to do this work and to consistently adhere to your schedule. Read one chapter a week and do the exercises that week unless you choose to spend more time on one chapter or another. The important thing is that you keep the momentum going. It takes at least three weeks to form this habit—to commit yourself to making this work a priority. Get your intentions clear to make this time a habit and become aware of the changes as they occur.

I recommend that you do the chapters in sequence instead of jumping around. They are designed for you to become gradually more and more self-aware, so that when you get to the more compelling areas of money and sex you will be ready. It is important to do the chapters in order because you are learning by doing, not just collecting information. As you go through the exercises at the end of each chapter you are laying the groundwork for what you will learn in the following chapter. You will be learning by increments, and each exercise will amplify the previous work as you move along. You will learn how to become more observant of the shifts in your behavior and how to maintain them.

Reading this book is not enough. Practice will make the difference. The exercises hold the key to making real changes in your life. You can alternate reading the instructions to each other or, if you wish, you can use my recordings available on audiotape or CD. If you are doing the exercises alone, you can make your own recording of the exercises or use mine. To order the recorded exercises, access www.pfti.org (or www.lovinginthehereandnow.org).

At the beginning of each exercise is a short warm-up you should do, which I call your barometer. Close your eyes and imagine either a barometer or a dial with numbers from 1 to 10. Let a number come to you that represents your comfort level with yourself, with 10 being the most comfortable and 1 being the least comfortable. Be sure to notice the number without criticizing yourself. Just notice it. Then do it a second time to rate your comfort level with your partner. At the end of the exercises do this again and just notice if there is a difference. This may seem strange to you at first, but just take a moment to calmly observe yourself. You will discover how easy it is to develop a special awareness of how you are responding to the outside world.

As you get further into this book, you may be tempted to skip this momentary inward journey, but I encourage you to keep doing it. When it becomes a habit for you, it will amplify your awareness of yourself in exciting ways. You will find it valuable as you become more and more aware of your own inner experience, and in turn, you will be surprised and delighted to discover that you have increased your mastery of yourself. This little habit will bring you a sense of ease with yourself, energy, and aliveness.

You will find much repetition of language in these exercises. This is done for a purpose: we learn by repetition. Repetition is practice. Practice can help you learn on unconscious levels. In doing so, you may discover that your unconscious is learning all by itself.

These lessons are to be done when you are not under the influence of alcohol or drugs because they induce altered states that interfere with the work. At the end of each exercise are tools to help you weave what you are learning into your everyday life and love.

Here are some general guidelines:

- This will be your time to be alone with each other. You will need an oven timer, two sets of different-colored index cards, a loose-leaf notebook with dividers and paper, a journal, and a pen for each person. You will also need a six-foot rope or a piece of clothesline, two different-colored balls of thick string or yarn, and six strips of different-colored Post-its. In addition you will each need a hand mirror.

- This time should be a special time alone with each other. There should be no distractions—no kids, no phones, no pagers, no television.
- You will need a special place that is only for you. It should be private, comfortable, and pleasant.
- Set the timer for each exercise or each part of the exercise.
- Read the exercise together or one can read it to the other.
- Do the exercise individually where indicated. Then write down your reactions and thoughts. Take whatever comes and just notice what your mind is doing.
- Be sure to allot equal time for each of you. Share with each other whatever you want. Respect your own and/or your partner's need not to share if the time is not right and if either one of you has a need for privacy.
- Set a time for the next session and commit yourselves to keeping this appointment.
- *IMPORTANT:* Only talk about your work together in this space and in your special time together. Outside of this time just let it go and let it percolate in your own mind.
- Write in your journal whatever comes up for you. Some of the tools at the end will give you suggestions on what to look for.
- Remember to check with your inner barometer from time to time during the week.
- Pay attention to the changes in your behavior.

The case histories in this book are an amalgam of the many individuals with whom I have worked. Because of confidentiality, all the details have been changed. I have tried to keep true to the spirit of these beautiful and courageous people. It takes commitment, boldness, and daring to bring joy into life; many of the people with whom I have worked have succeeded in doing that. I have learned from every one of them.

Why Hypnosis Is Your Best Tool for Change

What Is Trance?

Have you ever become so totally involved with something that you forgot everything else? Have you ever sat for hours on a beach, hearing the sound of the waves, staring at the sparkling water, oblivious to the passing of time? Have you ever accomplished something easily and well while being preoccupied with something else? Have you ever lost yourself in the rhythmic labyrinth of a piece of music?

Do you remember driving your car, your mind blank, your body relaxed and alert, your eyes fixed on the white line in the middle of the road, when you suddenly thought of something you hadn't thought of in years? Do you remember a time when your emotions were so intense that you felt the earth move under your feet and every detail of the moment became exquisitely etched in your mind and heart?

Have you ever had a difficult problem that you really couldn't resolve and you sat back with a sigh, stared out the window, thinking of nothing, when suddenly the solution became clear? Have you ever awakened from a nap with the solution to a knotty problem? Have you ever been with another person and each of you was totally in the moment? It was as if you were both on the same shimmering wavelength. Nothing was held back and all moved in perfect rhythm.

In all those instances you were in trance. Some people call it "focus"; athletes call it "flow." Whatever you call it, it is a state of highly focused attention. Positive trance is a creative state. It is when you are precisely attuned to your inner rhythm and move with it without conscious thought. Think of the baseball pitcher who stands on the mound and blocks out the crowds, the other players, and even the batter standing in front of him; all he focuses on is getting the ball into the catcher's glove. When you are in positive trance, you have a sense of inner knowing, you can solve problems or achieve results that your conscious mind might not have been able to.

We can also shift into negative trances. Negative trance is when we experience shock or unconsciously receive distressful suggestions. Our survival fears come to the surface and we feel disempowered, ambivalent, conflicted, unclear—we may even have the strange feeling that we are observing the scene from some other place, as if we were watching a film. In this state, we have no awareness of our adult abilities. It is as if we are so overwhelmed by our childhood feelings that we have amnesia for our competent selves. We think with the child-mind of fear and helplessness; those body-processsing networks are reactivated and we are triggered into replicating the patterns of the early experience. In that moment we are shifted into the helpless state of childhood and are driven by it unawares. It is called "state-dependent memory, learning, and behavior."

We all slip into negative trances at times. Have you ever experienced a sudden shock and your mind went blank? Sometimes we are catapulted into feeling as helpless as a little child, speaking in that tiny voice we had many years ago and feeling powerless to stop it. Another trigger may launch us into anger so strong we are blinded by rage. At other times the shock may be so great that we drift around in a blurred, distracted state for hours—sometimes even for days.

Have you ever been talking to your partner and suddenly feel invisible and inaudible as you watch your partner's face glaze over, the eyes staring into the distance at some unknown image? Chances are your partner is lost in thought and in time and is totally unaware that you are talking. Your partner has shifted into some kind of trance, probably related to an imprint that is not even conscious.

There are more effective ways for you to deal with this than becoming infuriated or taking it personally, which usually means you are reacting to your own imprint. Ricky, a nurse, waves her hands in front of her husband, John, and says good-naturedly, "Hello, out there!" or "Pilot to control tower, come in! What's the weather like?" One of my sons, Nick, interrupted himself in the middle of a story he was telling me as I was peeling carrots, and said, "And the cow jumped over the moon" to see if I was really listening. I still laugh about that. Milton Erickson would get people's attention by saying, "And another thing . . ." without having described the first thing. Spontaneous trances are part of our everyday experience. It is important that couples become aware of them and not take the shift personally because it probably refers to something that happened long before the couple met.

Becoming aware of when you are in trance and making the distinction between your positive and negative trance states is the most important thing you can learn in this book. When you learn how to recognize when you are in these states you can learn how to master them. By applying the lessons in this book to your everyday life you can enrich all your relationships.

You can experience many kinds of trances induced by hypnosis. You can relax into a trance—into that state you are in right before you drift into sleep or right as you are waking up. In the performer's trance and the athletic trance you can experience heightened awareness and total absorption in the moment. People use trance to control pain and to heal faster in pre- and post-surgery. People use trance in forensic hypnosis to access forgotten details of a crime that can then be validated in reality. People also use trance in psychotherapy to access forgotten memories and abilities. Highly suggestible people who shift into trance easily are singled out by stage hypnotists for entertainment purposes. Stage hypnosis is different from therapeutic or clinical hypnosis, but the ability to make use of suggestion is characteristic of all forms of hypnosis.

Alexander was one of my clients. He was a tall, white-haired, fifty-eight-year-old, well-spoken, successful CEO who was responsible for hundreds of employees. It was only in the presence of his supercritical wife, Nancy, that he went into negative trance. Whenever she berated him, he would become like a nine-year-old boy.

When Alexander was a child, his father abandoned him and his alcoholic mother, an abusive woman who often beat Alexander. She would brutally attack him verbally and physically, and then fall to her knees, sobbing, begging her son's forgiveness. Little Alexander could do nothing to protect himself from his mother's outbursts, so he would passively accept her abuse and wait for her rage to subside.

His behavior is very much the same in his marriage to Nancy. When Nancy lashes out at him for some reason or another, he just freezes and helplessly stares wide-eyed at her. His passivity enrages her even more; for some reason his silence terrifies her, and she becomes even more verbally abusive in an effort to get some kind of response from him. Both Alexander and Nancy would often fall into these negative trances, moving into automatic responses that neither was aware of nor could stop.

The key for them was becoming aware of when they were slipping into trance and learning how to shift out of it. To help them do this, I taught them about self-hypnosis.

What Is Hypnosis?

Hypnosis is the process by which a person moves into trance. Milton Erickson, M.D., a pioneer of medical hypnosis who redefined and demystified our understanding of how hypnosis can be used successfully, believed hypnosis occurs naturally through daily communication and defined hypnotic trance as a state of total absorption. When in a hypnotic trance, we receive information into a different part of ourselves, and thus our minds work differently with the information we take in. In hypnosis, we are working at a deeper and more powerful level of awareness, and we are less judgmental. Our conscious mind can sometimes block information or have difficulty processing it, but at this deeper level of awareness we can more easily understand and receive messages that can be the keys to healing.

Erickson was paralyzed by polio at the age of seventeen, but he taught himself to walk again through hypnosis. By tapping into his early memories of how he learned to walk, he was able to replicate the process. His later research expanded the use of hypnosis in medicine, dentistry, and psychiatry. He demonstrated that when people shift into hypnotic trance they open themselves to unconscious learning, which often impacts their bodies. In fact, there are observable physical changes that occur when one goes into hypnotic trance: breathing and pulse rates may slow down, muscles may relax, facial color may become heightened, pupils may dilate, eye fixation may occur, or the body may become more still (catalepsy).

Different people go into trance differently. Most people experience changes in their body experience, in their feelings, in their comfort, and in their awareness. People in light trance can be aware of where they are and can enjoy what they learn and can use. People in deeper trance often cannot remember what is said to them until some time later. People can be in trance with eyes open or closed. People can be relaxed and look asleep or they can be alert and focused, as are many performers and athletes in trance.

There are many studies of the effectiveness of medical hypnosis, and many people have been able to use it to diminish their anxiety and to facilitate healing. It is often used in the following ways: to strengthen the immune system, to minimize reaction to severe burns, to minimize reactions to powerful anticancer medication, and to control bleeding. It is used in pre- and post-surgery, in obstetrics, to control acute and chronic pain, and in dentistry. It is now being taught in many medical schools and has become more widely recognized by the medical establishment as a valuable asset and adjunct to medical care.

There have been hypnotizability scales that measure how suggestible to hypnosis a person is. Stage hypnotists are skillful at identifying highly suggestible people. The hypnotist goes through the audience and asks people to perform an exercise. He attempts to induce them into a trance and then may ask them to clasp their hands, suggesting that their hands are glued together. He then selects the people who cannot separate their hands because they will make the best demonstration subjects. People who test as "low suggestibles" can also be hypnotized, but it may take a little more time and more practice.

The traditional idea of hypnosis is that all of the power rests in the hands of the hypnotist, that it is the skill of the hypnotist that determines the success of the hypnosis. But Erickson believed that it is the ability of the unconscious to make use of the hypnotic suggestion that makes all the difference. Erickson used suggestive direct and indirect language to help people tap into their unconscious and reorganize and resynthesize their inner experience. Here the power is in the creativity of the subject's unconscious. The conscious mind is critical and screens out information. The unconscious receives information and can reorganize it according to the needs of the subject.

Hypnosis also helps us to dissociate, which means that we separate one part of our mind from another part: We are able to be in the present moment and at the same time experience a past memory that seems just as real. We are able to recognize that we are in a trance and, without judgment, recognize what triggered our automatic response. As suggested by Ernest Hilgard, Ph.D., this part of ourselves is called "the hidden observer"—a part of our mind that is always aware on a conscious and unconscious level.

I used hypnosis with Alexander, the CEO who reverted to his nine-year-old behavior around his domineering wife. First, using age regression, we went back to painful scenes in which his mother abused him physically and verbally. Alexander wept as he watched what that frightened little boy went through. With this newfound compassion, he became determined to protect that boy. I taught him techniques he could use to interrupt the trance. With practice, Alexander learned to use the feeling of dread that he associated with his mother's tirades as a trigger to shift himself out of his little-boy role and into his masterful and quick-witted adult self. Now, when his wife, Nancy, begins to berate him, he no longer is passive; he stands his ground.

Alexander's change of reaction brought about a change in his wife as well. Nancy had been a foster child, constantly shuffled from foster home to foster home. Through age regression, she remembered many painful scenes of adapting to a family and having to say goodbye. Alexander's silence had always triggered her feelings of abandonment, and her fear prompted her to act all the more angrily. Now that Alexander no longer retreated into silence, she could relax. And Alexander realized that Nancy wasn't his enemy, nor was she trying to hurt him; he now saw her as someone struggling with her own childhood issues. For years, they had been entering into negative trance together by triggering the unrecognized fears they both harbored. Now that they were able to recognize their lapse into trance, they were able to cut it off and relate to each other wholly in the present.

Hypnosis also was successful for my client Sally, whom I wrote about in the introduction. In hypnosis, Sally was able to track the helpless feeling she felt with her husband, Don, back to the forgotten scene in the boxing ring with her little brother. In hypnotic trance, she was able to go beyond the terrible fear she was feeling in the moment with Don, back to the plight of that little girl long ago. Because her adult self saw with a different perspective, she discovered that she felt genuine compassion for that little girl. The negative trance she had carried around with her came from her little-girl feeling that to please her father she had to let herself get beaten up. Not consciously aware of this behavior, she kept repeating it in her life. When she became aware, her compassion and caring integrated that little girl into her woman's heart. In effect, the mother part of herself took control and the child part could relax and feel protected.

▶ EXERCISE 1 ◀
SAFE PLACE

This is to help you program a safe place within yourself that you can shift into whenever you want or need to. Just by putting your thumb and forefinger together and taking a deep breath you can give the signal to your body to relax and your mind to become clear. It can be a haven of comfort in times of stress.

You may already have an inner resource of comfort, a place in your imagination you can retreat to in times of distress. If you don't, ask your creative self to make it up. You can change it as you wish. Some people design a special room that has everything they love in it. Others go to the beach or the mountains or a tree house they built as a child. Repeat this exercise as many times as you want, to "get it into your bones."

It is important that you let yourself experience this inner space with each of your five senses: smell the ocean; hear the sound of the crunch of snow; see the colors of the sunset; feel the grass under your bare feet; taste the cool, fresh water from a mountain waterfall. You will probably begin to feel your body react to your sense memories as you continue to practice. Repetition reinforces the installation of the pattern of associations linking your thoughts and your neurology so that the more you focus on what you see and hear and feel, the easier it is to let your body revivify those sensations. This pattern of associations will become so ingrained that in difficult situations, all you have to do is put your thumb and forefinger together and you will automatically experience a sensory reaction.

For example, if I have to go into a room of unfamiliar people and I am anxious, all I do is put my thumb and forefinger together and I smell the aroma of the lilac bush I loved to sit under every spring when I was a child, especially after a rainstorm when I could shake the branches and drops of lilac water would fall from the blossoms onto my tongue and into my eyes. As I smell the lilacs, my whole body shifts into a state of serenity mixed with an incredible energy, and it becomes a pleasure to meet new people as I walk into the room.

Creating your own safe place can be easy. Sit facing each other. Look at each other and notice your breathing. Notice what you are feeling as you look at your partner. You may want to laugh or cry, or you may feel a little anxious. Whatever you are feeling is just fine. Just notice it, like a cloud floating along the horizon of your mind, and then let it go and move on.

Close your eyes for a moment and check your inner barometer. Let a number come to you that represents your comfort level with yourself and then your comfort level with your partner. Let your thumb and forefinger on one or both hands come together, as if they were magnetized, and notice the exquisite delicacy with which they touch. As they touch, let them press harder until you can feel the pressure all the way up into your shoulders. Look up to the ceiling and take a deep breath, hold it for the count of five, 1 . . . 2 . . . 3 . . . 4 . . . 5 . . . and then, keeping your pupils looking up, let your eyelids close and your body relax into the support of the chair. And as your body becomes more and more comfortable, your mind can become more and more clear with each deepening breath you take.

And as you become more relaxed and comfortable, let yourself go to a safe place in your inner mind, a place where you feel secure and connected to life energy . . . to beauty and to feeling at home with yourself. If you cannot remember that safe place, make it up. You may have a favorite beach or garden, or perhaps a pond. You may like walking through the woods, especially in the winter, and feeling and hearing the crunch of snow as you move through the whiteness. And while I may be mentioning one safe place, you can be thinking of your own quite different place, and that is fine. Just be there for a few minutes and let yourself see what is there, hear the sounds, feel the texture of the air, smell it and touch whatever you need to. Then, when you are ready, come back to the room and open your eyes, feeling refreshed and comfortable. Notice your thumb and forefinger. Are they still touching? When you are ready, pick up your pen and your journal and write down whatever thoughts come into your mind. Take a few minutes to do that and then, if you would like, talk with your partner.

At the end of this exercise just close your eyes for a moment and check your inner barometer for your comfort level with yourself and with your partner.

▶ Tool Kit

During the week find an uninterrupted moment once or twice a day to just put your thumb and forefinger together and take a deep, comfortable breath and go to your safe place. Mel Bucholtz said, "It's a good idea to go into a mini-trance every once in a while just to remember you are alive!" Notice any changes in your behavior, even small changes.

► EXERCISE 2 ◄
SAFE PLACE LISTENING

After you have practiced the short version and have enjoyed playing with it, do this exercise. You can go to places in the past; you can go to places in the future; you can stay securely centered in the present. You can learn to use this in specific uncomfortable situations such as before a difficult confrontation or in the midst of a lot of confusion.

Relax into this uninterrupted privacy. Set the timer for ten or twenty minutes, as you choose. Sit opposite each other, with legs and arms uncrossed, eyes open or closed. Your body and, if possible, your neck should be supported so that you can relax into the feeling of letting go of the tension you may not always pay attention to.

Listen to your breathing; let it become deeper as you become more comfortable . . . and let each breath be a reminder to your inner mind to let go. This is to bring you to a point of focus, to maximize your ability to become clear and connected. Let your awareness move through your body and when you find a place that is tense, breathe warm, glowing air into it. Check your inner barometer for your comfort level with yourself and with your partner.

As you let yourself move into quietness, become aware of your own breathing and be curious to see if you are breathing with your partner. Don't force yourself to breathe with your partner, just notice when you do. It means you are more likely to be on the same wavelength. Just observe whatever is happening without judging.

Now put your thumb and forefinger about a half an inch from each other, becoming aware of the warmth between them. As you become more comfortable, notice how they can be drawn toward each other until they touch. When they touch, notice the delicacy of that connection, and then press them together until the pressure moves up into your shoulder blades. Take a really deep breath and let your whole body soften and relax, letting go of all that tension. Let your body feel as if you were floating on a cloud somewhere, while your mind grows more and more clear the more relaxed you become. Notice that your thumb and forefinger want to move gently apart or perhaps just touch a little.

Now let yourself go to some safe and comfortable place that you love, where you can feel completely at one with yourself and the whole universe. If you cannot yet remember that feeling, make it up just the way you want it. Now in your mind's eye, really see this favorite safe place, feel it in your body, on your skin, smell this place, breathe in the air, feel the texture of it. Let your body drink it in while your mind moves wherever it wants.

Let yourself *enjoy* this peaceful, serene moment. If you experience interrupting thoughts, like thunder somewhere, just let them be there and let your mind follow wherever it wants to go. You may learn something . . . and you may not. There is no right way. There is only your way. Meanwhile, let your thoughts move across the horizon of your mind like clouds and just observe them changing shape and sometimes dissolving.

If you would like, let your mind go back to something your partner said to you at some time or another that gave you a good feeling, that touched you, made you feel loved. Focus on one aspect of that moment—the look in the eye . . . the tone of voice . . . the sensitivity of the touch—and be with that feeling. Breathe it in. Let it fill your whole body.

Now let that feeling go and think of a time when you expressed a warm and loving feeling to your partner that you know made your partner feel loved. Get in touch with that part of you that knows how to do that . . . and breathe it in.

When you feel ready, let your eyes open. Notice your thumb and forefinger. Are they still touching? Perhaps look at your partner. Then write down whatever comes to mind about what you have just done.

Notice what you are writing and how you are feeling. Perhaps you are surprised or sad or reaffirmed. Perhaps you are disappointed or even angry that things have changed or that nothing really happened. Just notice what you are feeling and write it down.

Now set the timer and each of you take five minutes to share with the other whatever came up for you. Stop when the timer goes off. Only talk about this experience when you come together to read this book and do these exercises. Set up a time to do the next session.

▶ Tool Kit

Every day during the next week find an uninterrupted moment, put your thumb and forefinger together, take a deep breath, go to your safe place, and review moments in which someone said or did something that gave you a sense of warmth and pleasure, especially something you might not have noticed before. Notice whatever changes you experience. Write them in your journal if you want to.

Check your inner barometer for your comfort level with yourself and with your partner.

The Power of Imprints:
Why Do I Always Do the Same Thing
Even Though It Never Works?

The memories that we access in trance are actually memories we have received in trance during states of strong emotions. When we experienced distress as children, part of our minds—that wonderful part that works to protect us—caused us to dissociate from the moment. We went into trance and were able to distance ourselves from the abuse, from the feelings of rejection, abandonment, fear, anger, or shame. Although we were able to block those memories from our conscious awareness, they were recorded deeply within us. Similarly, moments that caused us to feel an overwhelming sense of love, acceptance, or security are also stored within us. These stored memories are called imprints.

We may go through our lives not consciously aware of these imprints, but our conscious awareness is just the tip of the iceberg. The unseen part—our unconscious imprints—move us through the time and space of our lives. Seemingly beyond our control (how can we control something we're not aware of?), our imprints cause us to keep repeating our past. When we experience strong emotions in the present, we shift into trance behavior and express not our true selves, but the adaptive part of ourselves that we developed in order to survive an emotionally difficult time in our past. We may even actually feel those childhood feelings as if we were still in that moment.

In positive trance we can access the feelings of our positive imprints and re-experience the love and joy that had such a powerful effect on us when we were children. In negative trance, feelings associated with traumatic moments surface, and the defenses our inner mind used to protect us at the moment of imprint are called to the fore in the present.

How many of us were imprinted by a critical parent or teacher and still have difficulty drawing or writing or speaking before a group? How many of us can remember the word or touch of one truly supportive person who encouraged and motivated us to accomplish our goals? These experiences can be in the back of our minds, long forgotten consciously, but still affecting the way we feel about ourselves when we find ourselves in situations that we associate with our earlier experiences at home, at school, or on the playing field.

More than forty years ago, someone corrected my pronunciation of "lingerie," and since then, whenever I have read or said the word, I always think of that person and get a twinge of that embarrassed feeling. I associate that person with that word and I still get that feeling of embarrassment—even forty years later.

Amy, like many young women, was in perpetual conflict between having a successful career and getting married to a successful man and having babies. An attractive, intelligent research fellow in anthropology with a wicked sense of humor, she really wanted it all, but her feelings about herself not being as smart as her younger sister and her terror of having a marriage like her parents' kept her from moving forward. Her mother, the daughter of a wealthy and aggressive manufac-

turer, had married a man from another country who was economi-
cally ineffectual and not on her social level. She had two children and
constantly complained to her daughter that her husband—Amy's father—was lazy, unambitious, and not bright—basically not good
enough for her. When she wasn't complaining about her husband, she
was complaining about her job as a nutritionist.

Amy's idea of men was imprinted by her mother's disappointment
and dislike of her husband and her resentment of her economic circumstances. Once in therapeutic hypnosis, Amy began to hear her
mother's voice every time she dated a new man. She also recognized
that it contributed to her dissatisfaction with her work. She became
painfully aware of her unconsciously absorbed belief that "life sucks."
As she tracked how this belief was affecting every part of her life, she
learned to counter it every time she became aware of it. She saw that
she had idealized her father to counter her mother's hatred of him,
and when he couldn't measure up to her pictures, she became enraged.
This pattern carried over to her relationships with men.

She began to recognize what *was* working in her life. She also discovered that she was not a carbon copy of her mother, that indeed she
was very different. She began to separate her own ideas from the unconscious roles she was living out—being responsible for her mother's
unhappiness and also being her mother's dependent little girl.

What made things even more difficult for Amy was that she
sought comfort in her mother whenever she experienced disappointment in a relationship or in her career. Every time she had a date with
a man who "didn't measure up" to her (unrealistic) expectations, Amy
found herself going to her mother's house, sitting on the family
couch, stuffing herself with potato chips, watching TV, and "numbing
out"—her child way of dealing with the pain she didn't want to see in
her mother. This denial of her mother's pain is a kind of emotional
blind spot that children develop when it is too hard for them to see
the suffering of a parent. Amy also felt on some level that to become

happier than her mother would be disloyal. It is a kind of negative trance in which the child feels helpless yet responsible for parental suffering. The feeling remains, but the awareness goes underground. It is too painful to see clearly. In times of pain, we revert back into this state, comforting ourselves as we did as children, relegating the imprints to the back of our minds.

Children are sensitized to their parents, their siblings, their teachers. The suggestions and impressions they take in are the imprints. Imprints become the nuclei around which we organize our behavior, our personalities, our relationships, and our feelings about ourselves. They usually remain buried and trigger repetitive behavior we have learned unconsciously.

Imprints occur when the child is in the absorptive state of unconscious learning, which we call trance. Children spend many hours in this state of learning. Their parents learned the same way from their parents. Hypnotic messages are passed down from one generation to the next. Parents are the unwitting conveyors of the unconscious messages that *they* learned as children. As a client said to me recently, "We don't do what our parents told us to do, we *are* who our parents were!"

These generational messages are tied to our innermost feelings of self-worth and self-esteem. Children need to feel loved in order to live emotionally healthy lives. Often, like Sally, who let her little brother beat her up in order to get her father's approval, they adapt to uncomfortable messages to please their parents. Sometimes we have conscious memories of these adaptations; often we do not. One client of mine, Nancy, a perfectionist who has held many unsatisfying jobs, was repeatedly told, "You never do anything right and you never will!" She couldn't enjoy anything she did because she was always afraid of making a mistake. Beverly, an economist, lived out her competitive mother's exhortation: "No man will ever want to marry you. You are too smart for your own good!" For many years she believed that she couldn't be smart and lovable because of that early imprint.

Children are easily influenced. They believe what is told to them about themselves, even when they sense it is not true. The message behind these statements, even if it is not consciously intended, is too painful for a child to take in, so we repress such imprints and then proceed to choreograph our lives around them. "Go make something of yourself," Marjorie was told, "so you won't have to do what I did— marry and be a slave to some man!" Marjorie, who owns her own dress shop, has been a workaholic who never has any time for herself. "My life is drab and joyless, like my mother's," she said when she came into therapy.

The messages we absorb are not only what we are told. We absorb what we see and sense, what we identify with on some level. The mind of a child absorbs unconscious messages so that what is *not* said is often more important than what *is* said. A little girl looks up at her angry mother's face, sees the clenched teeth, and hears the harsh voice. The mother says, "But I really love you!" The child will deny her own feelings about what she sees and hears because she needs to know her mother loves her at that moment. If it happens often enough, the child will begin to look outside herself for validation, for approval, rather than trust her own experience. When this happens her sense of herself is compromised. She cannot know her individual self because she is so busy looking outside herself for approval. She doesn't develop her own individual sense of her unique boundaries. She merges into other people's feelings about her, rather than listening to her own. She cannot trust who she is.

Children sense family secrets or family shame. Jack's family had escaped the Holocaust and emigrated to America. He always spoke in such a low, almost conspiratorial tone that it was hard to hear him. The invisible terror still seemed to surround him as he sat on the edge of his chair, almost afraid to relax. Invisible terrors can also surround the consciousness of people who have been physically or sexually abused. It is hard for them to relax into their bodies, and what a relief when they learn how to do that. Therapeutic hypnosis can free such people to learn to enjoy their own breathing. It seems simple, but it is not simple for people who have unconsciously been constricted in their bodies for a lifetime.

▶ EXERCISE 3 ◀
ACCESSING YOUR RESOURCES

Again, let yourself relax into this special space for just the two of you. Let a sense of comfort envelop you with each breath you take. The deeper you breathe, the more comfortable you feel . . . and the clearer your mind becomes. Close your eyes for a moment and check your inner barometer for your comfort level with yourself and with your partner.

Now each of you interlace your hands together and notice which hand is on top. Change their positions so that all the fingers that were interlaced below are now on top. Notice if there is a difference with how this feels. This nonhabitual interlacing handclasp is the clasp to use in the following exercise. Let your hands separate.

Put your thumb and forefinger together and let yourself go to your safe place (either the same one or a new one you can make up if you want to) and breathe in the sights, the sounds, the feel, the smell, and the taste of it.

When you are ready, go back to a time when you achieved something wonderful. It could be as simple as learning the letters A, B, C. It could be the first picture you drew, or how you discovered you could make purple by scribble-scrabbling blue and red together. It could be learning how to stand up, pulling yourself up and falling down, rolling over, sitting up, considering the situation, and pulling yourself up again and again until that one miraculous day when you lifted one foot and stayed standing!

And when you are with that memory of achievement, whatever it is, let your hands come together in that nonhabitual interlacing handclasp and really breathe in that feeling of accomplishment.

Let your hands separate. Now think of a time when you wanted to do something and were frightened or scared, but somehow you managed to do it anyway. It can be something very simple; it can be asking a question you were afraid to ask. If you cannot think of something, make something up. Let yourself go to that moment when you did something you were frightened to do and you managed to complete it, and look back and feel really good about yourself for being able to do something, even though you were scared.

When you are with that feeling of pride and accomplishment, again let your hands come together in that nonhabitual clasp and feel the moment and honor it with your silence, that healing space between thoughts. Then let your hands separate . . .

Now think of a time when you accomplished something and you didn't even know you had done it. It was so easy and so simple you surprised yourself and said, "I can't believe that I did this." And again when you are in touch with that particular feeling of surprise and delight, bring your hands together in the nonhabitual interlaced clasp and let yourself breathe in your delight at your accomplishment and honor it in silence.

Now let your hands separate again and think of a time when you wanted so badly to do something and somehow just couldn't do it the way you wanted. Something didn't work and you were disappointed, perhaps even in despair. Think of the part of you that was so upset at that time—perhaps it was a long time ago . . . perhaps it was recently. Let that part of your heart that has compassion and the ability to accept, forgive and feel tenderly toward your own dear self. Feel that feeling of compassion, and when you are in touch with that compassionate part let your hands come together in that particular way and breathe in the feeling of softness, kindness, and tenderness toward yourself. It may be a new feeling for you. . . .

Now let your hands separate and think of a time when you were with a group of friends and you all laughed when somebody said something really absurd—you know how kids belly laugh—and there was that crescendo of laughter and joy, and then it sort of faded out. Then someone giggled and all that laughter started again. Let yourself and your body remember that pure pleasure of shared belly laughter. When you are with that, again let your hands come together in that particular way and breathe it in.

Let your hands separate. Now, think of a time when you looked at someone you still love and suddenly realized just how much you loved him or her. There is a look, a tone of voice, a change of expression in their eyes that you really love. When you are with that feeling, again let your hands come together in that particular way and breathe that wonderful feeling in.

Now let your hands separate and think of a time when you were aware that someone you still love really loved you. Somehow they said something, or did something, or touched you and you felt fulfilled and loved. And when you are with that moment, perhaps long forgotten, again let your hands clasp together and breathe in that feeling. Let yourself experience that warm excitement . . . and then let your hands separate.

Now let your hands clasp together in that nonhabitual way and let yourself just be with yourself and the silence . . . enjoying the silence . . . enjoying being with all these parts of yourself and all these experiences and many others that are somewhere in the treasure chest of your mind. Take two minutes to enjoy being you, and then come back to the room, write down what occurs to you that you want to remember, that you can connect with. Close your eyes for a moment and check your inner barometer for your comfort level with yourself and with your partner. Then share what you are thinking and feeling with your partner.

▶ Tool Kit

During the following week notice moments when you feel good about something you have achieved, or are touched by someone you love, or laugh uproariously, and if you can remember, just let your hands come together in the nonhabitual clasp to anchor in that good feeling. Also, if there is a moment when you are really disappointed in yourself, take a moment and remember to have a little compassion for that part of yourself that can't always get it right and anchor that feeling of compassion. Notice any changes in your behavior. You might want to note these experiences in your journal.

▶ EXERCISE 4 ◀
USING THE ROPE

Let yourself get settled in your special place. Check your inner barometer for your comfort level with yourself and with your partner. Then discuss with your partner some minor disagreement that you have that you can argue about without going ballistic. If you are doing this exercise alone, go inside yourself and find two parts of yourself that disagree about something. For example, one part of you wants to accept the promotion you were offered by a company that you hate; the other part wants to find another job in a company you might like better. Stretch the rope out horizontally between you, each of you being on opposite sides. If you are alone, place the rope horizontally in front of you and determine which side represents the part of you that wants one thing and the part of you that wants something else.

This is an exercise about boundaries. In our relationships we often lose contact with our own feelings by trying hard to mind-read our partner. We lose connection with ourselves because we are so busy worrying about what the other person will think or do. Some of us are terrified of abandonment if we say what we really feel, so we spend our lives walking on eggshells. As children we learned to say what our parents or teachers wanted to hear, rather than express what we really thought or felt. That pattern persists into adulthood.

We also lose contact with our feelings when we seek to blame someone else. We focus on what the other person said, or did, or feels, because it is easier than examining and taking responsibility for our own words, actions, or thoughts.

Staying connected to our own feelings is not easy when we are upset. And when we are upset we very often blur our thoughts and feelings and judgments into one inflammatory statement. The rope between the two of you will help you remain connected to your own feelings and remind you not to step over the line into your partner's space.

When you say, "I think you don't know what you are talking about—as usual," you have stepped over the line into your partner's space. You have mind-read this person, since no one can really know what another person thinks no matter how long you have lived together. "You never listen to me" is also over the line; you're focusing on your partner's behavior instead of acknowledging how that behavior makes you feel.

"I feel invisible when you don't respond to me" is maintaining your own space. "I feel misunderstood" is staying with your own feelings. "I think you are stupid" is going over the line. Labeling and name-calling is always going over the line.

Before you begin the argument, put your thumb and forefinger together, take a deep breath, hold it for the count of five, and when you let the breath go, let go of any tension. Check your inner barometer for your comfort level with yourself and with your partner, and then stand up and look at your partner. If you are alone, take the role of each part of yourself in your inner conflict.

Set the timer for twenty minutes and then begin your argument. Each time either of you goes over the line, step over the rope then step back and say the same thing in a different way, staying on your side of the line by staying in contact with your own experience. Then continue the argument. You may want to score yourself on how many times you step over the line. As you become more aware of what you are saying, notice whether you stay more connected to your own experience and step over the line less often.

This is a valuable exercise in learning how to resolve arguments. It takes concentration and work, but when you relax it can become fun. You might even bring in a little humor once in a while and notice whether you use humor to step over the line with sarcasm or a little dig, or whether you can say something that gives you both a good laugh.

At the end of the exercise write down what you notice and then, if you wish to, share with your partner. Check your inner barometer for your comfort level with yourself and with your partner.

▶ Tool Kit

During the week, notice when you step over the line in your communication with your partner and others. Are you saying clearly what is your own experience or are you labeling or judging or blaming? Notice any changes in your behavior. Write in your journal whatever comes to you.

▶ EXERCISE 5 ◀
LISTENING AGAIN

Sit opposite each other. Each of you take two packs of the colored index cards to write statements on—one color for statements that make you happy, one color for statements that make you unhappy. Close your eyes for a moment and check your inner barometer for your comfort level with yourself and with your partner. Then relax into a deep breath and notice if you are breathing at the same rate as your partner. Let your thumb and forefinger come together and go to the safe place in your inner mind. Let yourself breathe ease and comfort into every cell in your body. Now think back over the week or perhaps the past six months and discover something your partner said to you that made you feel loved and warm inside. Write it down on your happy index card. Notice how you feel.

Now think of something your partner said that was not so comfortable, that may even have hurt your feelings. Write it down on the unhappy index card. Then turn it over and on the back of the card write what your partner could have said that conveyed the same message and would have been helpful to you. Now take a happy card and think of something helpful and loving your partner said to you and write it down. If it is difficult for you to shift back to the good feeling, just stop, put your thumb and forefinger together, and take a deep breath and go to your safe place for a moment and see if the good feeling comes back. If not, write the first memory down again.

When you are both ready, exchange the happy cards. Read the statements aloud to each other. You may want to talk about what you both felt. After a few minutes, sit back, relax, and take a deep breath.

When you are ready, exchange the cards that have the less comfortable statements on them. When you read the less comfortable words you spoke to your partner, notice how your breathing may change and see if you can keep it even and gentle as you turn the card over and read the suggested phrase that would have elicited a different response from your partner, while conveying the same information. Read the positive statement to your partner. Then when you are ready, exchange the second, happy cards and notice how you feel as you read them. Take five or ten minutes to talk about what you have discovered. Close your eyes for a moment and check your inner barometer for your comfort level with yourself and with your partner.

At the end of this exercise, please record the statements and suggested statements in your journal together with any reactions you may be having.

▶ Tool Kit

During the week you may notice that you are becoming more aware of how you are using language and how others, especially your partner, are responding to it. Notice this. Perhaps think of how you might say something differently. Jot it down in your journal.

3

Breaking the Code:
Understanding
Your Family Trance

Every family is unique. Each has its own rules, attitudes, secrets, and myths. Every family has its own patterns of coping with the stresses, strains, disappointments, losses, successes, and joys of living. Often these patterns can be traced from one generation to another.

Families are also imprinted by culture and cultural myths. Movies and television often depict a bumbling and not-too-intelligent father/husband who is the butt of family jokes. Yet the heritage of our patriarchal culture is that men are better and smarter, which is reflected in the economic metaphor of the glass ceiling. Many families harbor both myths simultaneously.

Religion can affect families profoundly as well. Certain religious traditions give strong messages about sexuality and what is "moral" behavior. Women, especially, may receive the message that sex is "dirty" or "something bad girls do." And these imprints become problematic when these women try to have healthy adult sexual relationships.

Families are also imprinted by world events, such as economic depression, war, and the Holocaust. Family legends, secrets, and humiliations have a powerful effect, too. An illustrious, strong matriarch or patriarch can imprint the family for generations to come.

Each family has its own language—conscious and unconscious—woven into the minds of all its members from generation to generation. We learned to speak by hearing words spoken to us over and over again. Unlike the inner process of learning how to walk, learning to speak comes from the external world—the words, phrases, and tones of voice we heard shaped our perception and our image of ourselves in relation to others. Unconsciously we learned to "read" voice tone, facial expressions, and body behavior. Our family consciousness was our introduction to the world.

But this family consciousness or language can be problematic as we relate to those outside the family. This is especially true in intimate relationships. Each member of a couple brings his or her family language into the relationship and the unrecognized and unresolved issues on both sides can drive the couple onto a collision course.

When we fall in love many of our negative imprints come in to focus. We tune in to each other on the same frequency that we tuned in to our parents and siblings when we were children. All the freshness and intensity of childhood—the excitement, the eroticism, the fear, the expectations—come into play. But also, all those buried negative feelings of childhood are stirred up. We begin to look to our partner to satisfy our unfulfilled expectations of childhood. We try to relate to our partner with our family language, but it's foreign to anyone outside the family. Our partner speaks his own language. Over time, we become deadlocked; our needs remain unmet and our relationship starts to crumble.

Larry and Louise unknowingly brought their family imprints into their relationship and were heading toward disaster. In working with hypnosis they focused on one experience that kept repeating itself. Louise always interrupted Larry, no matter what he was doing or saying. Larry hated it and would withdraw.

Larry, a psychologist, was the youngest of eight children. His mother never left him alone. Louise, a teacher, came from a large family, too. In her family love was expressed by everybody's joining in and interrupting each other, and finishing each other's sentences.

In hypnosis Larry remembered a moment of happily playing with his truck when his mother called him to dinner. He was so absorbed that he didn't answer her. She marched in angrily, swooped him up without a word, and plopped him down at the dinner table. He recognized that this was one example of his mother's insensitivity to his needs. As a toddler, he was enraged but could say nothing. As he grew up, he forgot his three-year-old rage at being interrupted, but his nervous system remembered.

Larry and Louise loved each other, but Larry got extremely annoyed whenever Louise interrupted him—which he said was constantly. Conversely, Larry's need to finish what he was absorbed in doing hurt Louise. She felt like he was rejecting her. She wanted to spend time together. Her father had been distant and rejecting; her mother was always available. She wanted Larry to act like her mother and felt the old pang of being pushed away by her father every time Larry, grim-faced, asked her to wait until he was finished. She usually insisted and he, with gritted teeth, usually interrupted what he was doing to join her at whatever she was doing. Larry resented the interruption, and Louise, even though she got what she wanted, was usually hurt and disappointed with his reluctant participation. Both were dissatisfied with the relationship.

In a session together, each remembered in hypnosis the forgotten painful imprints that were part of their family of origin. Those moments had gone underground, consciously forgotten, but had powerful influence on their lives. When those triggers were activated, both would slip into their family trance, reactivating patterns that were firmly established in their families. As she watched him in hypnosis, Louise was able to see that Larry was feeling an age-old intrusion, rather than deliberately trying to hurt her. She then had to learn how to shift out of her little-girl-rejected-by-father trance whenever Larry expressed a desire to complete a task before becoming engaged in an activity with her. Larry worked on dissolving his little-boy intrusion response so he could shift into a more receptive adult mode. Freed from the painful imprints, they both could then work on new ways to hear each other and respect each other's feelings. The pattern had been entrenched for a number of years, so they needed to work with each other over time to dissolve it for good. When they each experienced the pain in the other's intense imprinted response, they could begin to laugh at past disagreements and reframe future moments. The old sting had been removed and they each could handle the present difficulty and not turn it into a past childhood wound.

Dismantling Family Patterns

We all fall into a family trance from time to time, slipping into a role that we developed as children. Our task is to become aware of the triggers that reactivate those roles for us, and learn how to shift out of those patterns that were frozen in place in the past—before they disrupt our present and derail our future.

Tom and Debbie were a young couple whose happy marriage had been going down an increasingly rocky path. They had been married three years and had a five-month-old daughter. The relationship started falling apart after the birth of their baby.

Sometimes family trances become extremely pronounced when a couple has a child. The child-rearing process can activate our own childhood imprints and throw us back into situations we thought we had left firmly in the past (or weren't even consciously aware of). This is what happened to Tom and Debbie.

It was their anniversary and they went to their favorite restaurant for an elegant dinner. They raised their champagne glasses at the same moment, gazing deeply into each other's eyes. Although they were probably unaware of it, they were breathing simultaneously, speaking softly to each other in the same tone of voice and the same rhythm. They were seeing, hearing, feeling only each other, just as they did when they first fell in love—and into a love trance. Debbie began to get aroused. The memories of Tom's caressing her evoked feelings of excitement, of heightened awareness. Debbie started thinking about what their lovemaking would be like later that night. Would Tom gently undress her first? Meanwhile, Tom was thinking about how Debbie's face softens when he moves on top of her. He felt a stirring in his groin. Both were experiencing physiological changes. They were in trance; they were absorbed in each other—two people in a special and intimate relationship. It was as if their hearts were beating as one, and every cell in their bodies was resonating to the connection with each other.

Then Debbie suddenly put down her glass. She had an interrupting thought. She looked at her watch and said, "Oh, Tom, I'm sorry, I have to call the baby-sitter. I forgot to tell her what to feed Annie." Tom scowled, took a swallow of champagne, and said coldly, "Why is it every time we have some time alone lately you forget something and have to run to the telephone. It never fails! The baby-sitter will figure out what to feed Annie. Annie won't starve!"

Debbie's pupils dilated. She flushed. She got so angry she couldn't think straight. Doesn't he understand that she is now a mother and has responsibilities? Tom's sudden coldness triggered her memory of her supercritical mother. Debbie is convinced that she loves her baby more than her mother ever loved her.

Tom's sudden change of voice tone and facial expression shifted

Debbie into a long-forgotten experience when she was three years old and her mother screamed at her. She was unprepared and vulnerable; her body was flooded with helplessness and fear. Twenty-five years later, Tom's look triggered that same feeling, and she shifted into the trance she had entered as a three-year-old. Her physiology shifted, too. She was overcome by the same feelings, the same internal hormonal changes she experienced when her mother yelled at her and threw her whole nervous system into shock.

Debbie started to cry as Tom just stared at her. Somewhere in the back of his mind, concealed from consciousness, was the picture of his mother sobbing as his father bellowed while he, at age four, stood by, helplessly watching. Tom threw down his napkin, sat back, and glared. His temperature dropped, his circulation constricted, his chest muscles contracted, and his breathing became rapid. Less oxygen got to his brain, and he couldn't think straight.

Debbie rushed off to the ladies' room and Tom gulped down his champagne, debating whether to call for the check, take her home, and forget the whole thing, or sit in silence choking down a very expensive dinner. When Debbie, eyes still red, returned to the table Tom just stared at her, restraining himself so he wouldn't explode.

This is a typical example of what often happens with couples at some time or another. Tom and Debbie shifted into automatic pilot. Neither could understand how they had gotten into this argument, especially on their anniversary. In the intensity of the moment, they moved from a loving connection into a negative trance, words and expressions triggering an early-learning state of which they were not conscious. Yet they experienced it fully. Their bodies were totally involved in recoil. That night they lay back to back, each sleeping fitfully.

In therapy, Tom and Debbie learned to bypass the triggers that set off the old wounds by becoming aware of their inner states that are so sensitive to each other that they revivify the old scenes unknowingly. Becoming aware of the old scenes is the key.

Debbie learned to take a deep breath when she saw "that look" on Tom's face. In that moment she could quiet her anxiety and think clearly. Tom learned to recognize Debbie's anxiety and gently take her hand and comfort her. They both learned to sidestep their patterns and to melt the high drama into the next glass of champagne and create the preliminary to a beautiful night of lovemaking.

This kind of awareness takes practice; the reaction patterns have been there a long time. Some married couples evoke these patterns in each other year after year until their set responses become so familiar and repetitive that they forget there was ever another way—or that they ever really loved each other. The sooner you can interrupt the patterns the better, but it's never too late. *If there is still enough left in your relationship to motivate you to commit yourselves to doing the work, you can begin to recognize your triggers and dismantle them.*

Using the Genogram to Break the Family Code

John came to see me saying he felt "torn apart." He worked in a prestigious financial firm and was effective and successful, having risen to become a senior vice president. But he hated every minute of his work. Each time he was promoted he felt burdened by detail, pressured all the time, not particularly well liked, and basically lonely and isolated. He then came home to a cold and withholding wife who complained that he never paid attention to her. Their sex life was nonexistent and he saw no joy anywhere.

We did detective work, using a genogram to explore his family history. A genogram tracks family myths, rules, and messages against a background of social, historical, and interpersonal events. (Later in this chapter I will give you instructions for creating your own genogram.) Going back three generations, John began to see how his role as perfect peacemaker was played out by his father and great-grandfather in each of their families of origin and transmitted down to him. In hypnosis he saw how he was re-creating his childhood self-image, consciously *and* unconsciously every day at the office, unaware of all the feeling he was repressing and suppressing in order to stay in the family trance.

In his family of origin, his father and older brother fought constantly while his mother stood by and watched, tight-lipped and silently critical of her husband. John's older brother was unruly and out of control, and although his father argued with him, he never really stood up to the boy. Early on, to get his passive father's attention, John took the role of family peacemaker and the "perfect son" in contrast to his rageful brother. John saw that he had been playing the same part daily in the office, holding together the divergent groups and being the office "diplomat." He was chronically exhausted and was beginning to have chest pains, perhaps an indication that his heart was not in it. He was well on the way to passing along his family role to his middle daughter, the smartest of his three children and a perfectionist like himself.

John wept when he saw himself as a young boy trying desperately to keep the peace and recognized that his fear of "World War III" in his current family kept him in the stance of controlling everything around him at home also. There was no place to relax or be himself, since he hardly knew who he was anymore. His wife, Heloise, did not support anything he said or did.

The first thing John found helpful was the "safe place" exercise, and he began doing it for a minute or two during the day and in the evening. When he explored his little-boy feelings about his parents, John began to see that he constantly tried unsuccessfully to gain his mother's approval. He was now trying to get that approval from his withholding wife, an endeavor he realized was futile. He also realized that the woman he married was a lot like his mother: silently critical, complaining, and dissatisfied. These qualities had been so much a part of his life as a child that he had a blind spot about them and was unaware that it was these very qualities that had unconsciously attracted him to Heloise, because they were so familiar. He also discovered that he did not want to be like his father, whom he saw as being meek.

When John did his genogram he also discovered facts about his grandparents that he hadn't known. His paternal grandfather had been a prestigious judge from a small town who dominated his wife and four children, especially his oldest son, John's father. This explained John's father's timidity and inability to control his household. John's brother took on his grandfather's role as the family bully in reaction to his own father's ineffectualness. This was a long-standing family pattern. He tried to dominate everybody, especially his father and mother. John had to fill the void left by his ineffectual father and was the only one who could control his brother, at great cost to his own self-expression.

John went through the painful process of understanding that his father could not accept that John filled the void that his own passivity had created. He saw John as a competitor and could not accept him in the way John longed for. John also realized that the only person he could turn to was his critical mother. He used hypnosis to go back to many moments when, as a little boy, he had had to adapt to and placate his brother and his mother. In developing compassion for that sensitive little boy who was still sitting in his mind and heart, he began to honor other feelings he had within himself. He became more accepting of his need to placate and perform for his father, to be the "good son." His genogram helped him see the patterns he had fallen into and how he was replaying what had happened many generations before.

The genogram is a simple but powerful device to put together the often confusing and blurred histories of people who have come before us. Patterns, even obvious patterns, can be elusive. Little children sense something incongruous and then develop emotional blind spots to protect themselves from seeing what their as-yet-undeveloped nervous systems cannot tolerate. John could neither see nor comprehend the role he was programmed into. He just adapted because that was all he could do.

Children sense undercurrents and feelings, but avoid seeing what is in front of them because it is too painful. These childhood blind spots were emotional survival tools at the time. They often slip back into the unconscious and continue to blind us as adults so that what others may see clearly, we may not see at all.

Like John, you can learn to see your life against the background of the historical events (wars, depressions, loss of economic strength), family secrets, family fears, and the inevitable tragedies and losses that we all sustain in life. You can track family myths, messages, and secrets (constructed "to protect the children"), and you can discover family personalities and learn that their impact on their children can be a source of strength and resilience as well as weakness.

By seeing and experiencing his family-trance patterns, John was able to change his behavior at certain emotionally critical and stressful moments. He surprised (and delighted) even himself as he let go of the need to control at all times. At first it caused some consternation at the office and with his family, especially his wife. They all had gotten used to his taking charge and had gotten comfortable with ceding responsibility to him. But John's new behavior had powerful benefits for him. He could experience moments of authentic joy in his own abilities. People respected him more and his life expanded. He directed himself toward his deepest hopes, wishes, and goals, without finding himself losing control as his brother had or shutting down like his father. He discovered his own way by seeing clearly what he had only previously sensed—his reenactment of the family drama. He could breathe freely when he could sit in his own safe place and be himself.

As a psychotherapist, I do a genogram with every client because I feel responsible for our getting a sense of what his or her family consciousness is about and how it expands and/or restricts my client. In taking a family history, I ask for at least six adjectives for every family member and people who have influenced the life of my client, and a description of themselves, as they see themselves and as they think other people see them. How people define others says a lot about how they define themselves. I often have clients tell me a sentence or two that each significant member has said to them, something that the client has strong feelings about. We move into listing the family rules, secrets, rituals, and unconscious assumptions. Most important, we look for strengths in the family: moments of joy, play, fun; moments of mutual support; moments of selfless sharing. Moments of connection sustain us all and it is important to discover them, to revivify them and be able to access them whenever we need them—especially when we feel ourselves shift into discomfort and stress.

Often I will ask clients to give me a chronological list of decisions that were important in their lives—about how to get what they needed, about relationships, about how to get love and be loved, about the world, about the family they lived in. These decisions are most often a response to experiences in their families.

Favorite characters in nursery rhymes, children's books, movies, cartoons, songs, hopes, wishes, dreams can all contribute clues to an accurate picture of who a person is and what has shaped his life.

I often give my clients a list of suggested questions to use in the exploration of their family-of-origin history. Some clients have tape-recorded interviews with old uncles and aunts, many of whom are delighted to share long-forgotten family memories. Some people discover family members they didn't know they had. Others in their detective work come upon family secrets that suddenly clarify many family mysteries. Often people from the past come alive in their fragility, their strengths, their humanity. There can be a sacred feeling in fleshing out the people we came from in all their diversity and color, failures and successes, loves and hates. Many people feel a renewed sense of continuity and pride in the families they came from. People will explore their families individually or in "Family Reconstruction Groups," in which a group of people come together weekly or monthly to discover and role-play the unconscious patterns of their families of origin.

I suggest that you do the first three exercises this week and the next two the following week. They are designed to give you new perspectives on the old family themes so that you can enrich your conscious and unconscious knowledge of the people and places you come from.

▶ EXERCISE 6 ◀
DOING YOUR FAMILY GENOGRAM

Notes on Genogram

Chronological History

On the left side of the family map list all the historical events that occurred during the lifetimes of your family members. These events, as well as cultural and sociological influences, had direct or indirect influence on their life experiences and choices.

Family Events

- Marriages are shown horizontally, males on the left, females on the right.
- Birth order is shown vertically; birth dates and differences in years between siblings are shown.
- Chain of hearts connecting two people shows a loving relationship.
- Chain of crosses shows a hostile, antagonistic relationship.

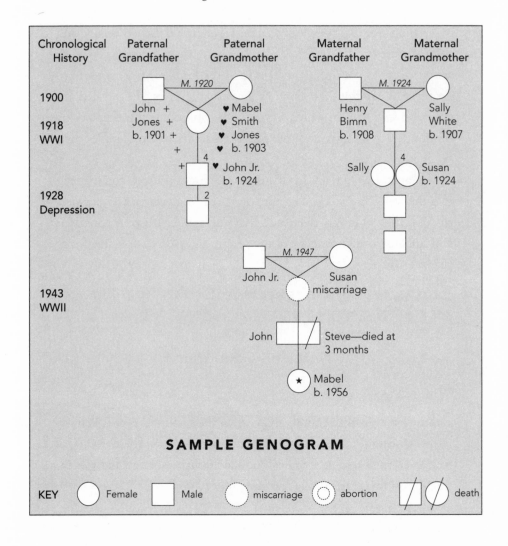

SAMPLE GENOGRAM

KEY ⬤ Female ⬛ Male ⬤ miscarriage ◎ abortion ▨ ⊘ death

- The star indicates the subject or subjects.
- Each person's family of origin is aligned above him or her.

Close your eyes for a moment and check your inner barometer for your comfort level with yourself and with your partner.

When you are ready, look at the sample of the family genogram shown above. Do your own family-of-origin genogram using the sample as a suggestion. It doesn't have to be perfect. Remember, every circle and square you draw represents a whole human being, a birth, a death, and all the struggles, triumphs, losses, and joys of human life. Go back at least two generations, to great-grandparents, or further if you want to. You may have been unconsciously influenced by stories about a distant relative who made a profound imprint on subsequent family generations. Notice how you feel as you are doing it.

Take another piece of paper and write down six adjectives for each of the people on your genogram. You may have some ancestors that you didn't know so just write whatever comes to your mind.

When you have finished, sit back, close your eyes, and just be with yourself and what you have just done. Then take a few minutes to write down whatever comes to your mind.

When you are ready, share with your partner.

▶ Tool Kit

During the following week take a few minutes occasionally to jot down any thoughts or associations that may come to you that have been stimulated by your work with the genogram. You may want to look at the genogram and add any new thoughts or information that come to mind. Notice any changes in your behavior and/or attitudes.

When you are ready, share with your partner.

▶ **EXERCISE 7** ◀
YOUR CHARACTERISTICS AND
WHERE THEY CAME FROM

Get comfortable as you sit facing your partner. Let your body become more and more relaxed. You can become exquisitely aware of your feet resting on the floor, and perhaps the feeling of the skin on the bottom of your feet next to your shoes or your stockings, or, if your feet are bare, the feeling of the texture of the floor. You might also become aware that deep in the center of the earth is a force that holds us to this planet, and that when you are fully connected to the floor, you can become more connected to that gravity force that can move up through your body. We are always grounded by the very power of gravity that holds us to the planet.

Close your eyes for a moment and check your inner barometer for your comfort level with yourself and with your partner. As you begin to move your thumb and forefinger together, become even more aware of the depth of your breathing, knowing that the more comfortable you become, the deeper your breath can go. As you breathe in, bring into your body the nutrients, oxygen, and life energy that can move into every system of your body, strengthening your immune system and enabling your mind to become more and more clear as your body becomes more and more comfortable.

Then let yourself move again to that safe place, or perhaps you want to find a different safe place from the one you already have. That is up to you. Let yourself really be there with all your senses: smelling this safe place, tasting it, touching it, letting the air move throughout your body, breathing in whatever it is that gives you the sense of being at home with yourself. Perhaps it is the salt air of the ocean, or you may be thinking of somewhere else. Maybe it is the smell of pine trees in the woods, or of newly mown grass in the spring, or the clear air after a rainstorm. You may love the movement of skiing, or riding a bicycle, or swimming—whatever gives you that sense of being fully alive in your body and at the same time relaxed and totally comfortable. Some people like to move through a garden and can actually smell the difference between a rose, a stargazer, a peony, a lilac. Let yourself go wherever you need to go to become more and more comfortable within yourself.

Sometimes you can be interrupted by your own doubtful thoughts, and that is part of the process. Let them be there, and notice when they disappear. Then let your mind go to some of your own thoughts about yourself, things that you like about yourself, maybe five or six characteristics or abilities or resources that are part of you. Focus on some part of yourself that you like—maybe it is your love of order, maybe it is your honesty, stubbornness, persistence, ability to laugh, ability to love, spontaneity, discipline; focus on whatever characteristic fits for you.

Maybe you can pinpoint how you came to have that special quality. See if you can associate it with some family member whom you like. Maybe you learned about that quality from that person. Some people say that personality characteristics skip a generation, so you might like to go back to a grandmother, grandfather, granduncle, or grandaunt whom you liked in some special way. You may go way back to a long-dead family ancestor who had a special personality. Take a minute of clock time to pinpoint how you came to have that special quality, perhaps something someone said, perhaps some way you responded to a special human being. Take two, three, or even four minutes more to let your mind focus on the qualities within you. Are you noticing something really extraordinary in some part of you? Maybe it didn't come from someone else. Maybe it is that special, sacred part of you. Then when your mind says, "Oh no, that's not me," let that be there. And go back to that quality that you were attracted to—maybe even secretly—in yourself and invite that quality to be there.

After you have explored these characteristics within yourself, go back in time when you were little and, if you can, get the sense of someone else who had this quality. Then let yourself come back to where you are in your special room and write down whatever comes to mind. After you have written down what you want, take five or ten minutes to share with your partner what you discovered and your feelings about it.

Close your eyes for a moment and check your inner barometer for your comfort level with yourself and with your partner.

▶ Tool Kit

During the coming week see if you can catch a thought or two about one of the people you identified with in this exercise and write it down. Notice any changes in your behavior and write them down also.

▶ **EXERCISE 8** ◀
SPECIAL PEOPLE IN YOUR LIFE

Sit comfortably facing each other, perhaps noticing something interesting about your partner's face or eyes that you may not have really seen before, or may have seen and forgotten a long time ago. Close your eyes for a moment and check your inner barometer for your comfort level with yourself and with your partner.

Then pick up your pen and your journal. List the names of the members of your family of origin and others—uncles, aunts, grandparents, even teachers or ministers, rabbis, or priests—who had a strong influence on you. List them in order of their importance to you and do it spontaneously, without thinking too carefully about it. Just take what you get. Go back over the list and write down the first six adjectives that come to you about each of those people. Notice the patterns, if there are any. Notice one characteristic you have seen in several people. Notice the similarities and differences and then notice what you are feeling as you go along.

The above is preliminary to a meditation that you can repeat many times with infinite themes and variations, with different people from the same stages of your past, or with the same people at different stages of your life. We all move and change and grow. What you may have felt and learned at one time may not be the same as what you have felt and learned at another time. Sometimes in meditation you see an experience from a different perspective and you may be surprised and delighted to learn something new about yourself or others, or you may see for the first time new meaning in an experience.

Now let your thumb and forefinger come together and take a deep, full breath. Count to five and as you let your breath go, move easily and gently into your safe place and breathe in that safety and security.

When you are ready, let a screen come up in front of your eyes or in the back of your mind. Now let a scene—a photograph from your family of origin, the people with whom you shared your life when you were little—come onto that screen. You may come up with a particular scene, perhaps long forgotten, that has some meaning for you. Let the scene become really clear and then turn it into a movie. You can be behind the camera, if you like, and zoom in on that movie, or zoom way back so that the film becomes very small, because you are in control.

Continue to watch the scene, and when you are ready, focus on one person from this family of yours who had great influence on you. Let your own unconscious do the choosing. You may have something you would like to say to that person that you never said, or you can imagine what that person may have wanted to say to you but couldn't. Notice what you are feeling now, and notice what you may have been feeling a long time ago at that particular moment in the film. Is it different?

Take a few moments until you feel you have completed this part of the exercise. When you are ready, open your eyes and write in your journal whatever you want and then share with your partner.

When you are done, check your inner barometer for your comfort level with yourself and with your partner.

▶ Tool Kit

Again, during the week notice thoughts you may be having about the person or persons you remembered in this exercise and write down your impressions. Also, write down any changes in your behavior you have noticed.

Hypnotic Experience in Everyday Living: Getting Rid of the Ghosts

We are continuously shifting our states of awareness as we move through our days and nights. Paul MacLean, senior scientist and former chief of the Laboratory of Brain Evolution and Behavior at the National Institutes of Health in Bethesda, Maryland, says there are three separate and distinct functioning parts of the brain—the neocortex, which is the "thinking, see-hear-feel brain"; the limbic or emotional brain; and the earliest brain, the reptilian or the basic brain, which is also called the survival brain. He says that the brain functions on these three levels in discrete and organized ways: Each of the three functioning parts of the brain follows its own rules.

Radically different chemistry and structure and in an evolutionary sense countless generations apart, the three neural assemblies constitute a hierarchy of three-brains-in-one, a triune

brain. . . . Stated in popular terms, the three evolutionary for-
mations might be imagined as three interconnected biological
computers, with each having its own special intelligence, its
own subjectivity, its own sense of time and space, and its own
memory, motor, and other functions.

The "whole" is greater than the sum of its parts, because
the exchange of information among the three brains means
that each derives a greater amount of information than if it
were operating alone.

—Paul MacLean, from *The Three Faces of Mind*,
Elaine de Beauport, p. xxii

What is important for us to understand with regard to the shifts of
our states of consciousness is that the deepest level of the brain, the
reptilian brain, is the source of the survival instinct—the fight-or-
flight response. It is the spinal cord and brain stem, the part of us that
is rooted in our need for structure. It is this part of the brain that is
imprinted by trauma because it is rooted in our primitive need for
protection. In an evolutionary survival sense, this cold-blooded reptile
within us moves toward and away from its perception of danger.

This basic brain can function in negative and/or positive ways. Remember Abraham Curtis, who held on to the headache for twenty-
five years until his basic brain received the suggestion in trance that
the war was over and he no longer needed the headache to prevent his
going back to the front? He was freed from the "protection" of this
part of his mind and got on with exploring and evolving his life. There
are psychological pains that people struggle with for years because the
survival part of their mind is trying to "protect" them.

We need to understand this reptilian part of our brain because it
often forms the basis of the life choices we make. When it gets imprinted by trauma, it organizes against any repetition of that trauma.
On an unconscious level it stands guard, ready to react to the slightest

threat. This powerful part of our minds virtually rules our lives. Whenever we try to achieve something and have a pattern of failure, it is our "reptilian brain" that paralyzes us. Here are two examples: when we are in a job that is not fulfilling but we cannot leave it; when we are in a relationship that we long to free ourselves from, yet we cannot move. When we can observe this part of our mind's focus on our survival, we can understand much more about ourselves. Even the anticipation of pain, which is often unconscious, is enough to keep us in a pattern of failure.

When we shift into the state of consciousness called trance, we come closest to accessing ways of thinking and feeling that are rooted in this primitive basic brain. In hypnosis, the negative unconscious patterns that have been imprinted there can be evoked and positive changes can be introduced. This is why hypnosis can help us. This is why we need to recognize when we go into trance so we can imprint positive messages. Revivifying a joyful imprint of childhood can amplify the experience, bringing it into present consciousness to lay the groundwork for new ways to relate to the self and to life.

As Paul MacLean notes, the whole brain is greater than the sum of its parts, and I believe it is in this whole brain that profound change and transformation takes place. Knowing when we shift into spontaneous or suggested trance, and observing without judgment the movement of our thoughts and feelings when we are in this state, creates the possibility for pattern change. We may not always know consciously how we are moving into that change, but we *can* know that something within us is happening at this level. When we are in this deepest level of communication with our own mind and we recognize patterns and heretofore unavailable associations is when we can open the door into new realms of experience for ourselves. Often when we pray, meditate, or go into self-hypnosis, we can enter this level of brain function.

Hypnotic Triggers in Everyday Living

There are triggers that can shift us into negative or positive trance. Everyday triggers can be certain "buzz" words. When Sandra was six, she wanted to become a ballerina but was told, "You dance like an elephant." She stopped her dancing lessons and for thirty years, whenever anyone mentioned the word "elephant," she suddenly felt inconsolable sadness. For all those years she hated her body. Looking at it from her adult perspective in hypnosis, Sandra saw that the offending person was the mother of a little girl who couldn't dance as well as she could. But as a child, Sandra was so shocked and hurt at the statement that her mind took it in as the truth.

Sometimes people can suddenly feel "down." When they think back, they often find a trigger, as a client of mine named Susie did. Her mother constantly called her "selfish and self-centered like your father" so that every time Susie was told she had to learn to be selfish and to stand up for herself, she would feel her stomach go into spasm.

We are affected by positive triggers, too: somebody's name; a song you used to sing; a picture of an old haunt; the aroma of a lilac branch or of perfume or aftershave worn by someone you love.

We can learn to recognize the triggers in our family activities: on holidays, in the rituals of anniversaries, births and birthdays, deaths and funerals, family jokes, family arguments, family milestones.

There is also a physiological component. Johnny was eating shrimp the night his parents told him they were getting divorced. Although he had never been bothered previously, he discovered that eating shrimp caused him to break out in hives and he has not dared to eat shrimp since.

When I was little, my family left a box of candied fruit in a windowsill in the living room. The colors were so beautiful and the sugar tasted so good that I am told I ate the whole box and became extremely ill. I don't remember eating it, but to this day the smell of candied fruit or of orange marmalade makes me intensely nauseous. I probably could use self-hypnosis and visualize that candied fruit on top of a big piece of chocolate cake and use it as a trigger to stop eating cake, but I think there are better ways to restrain oneself (besides, do I really want to give up chocolate cake?).

The problem for most people is they don't know when they have shifted into their child (or family) trance state so they can't shift themselves out of it. The keys are:

- to recognizing this state as you move into it;
- to identify the triggers that cause it;
- to shift out of these feelings;
- to use hypnotic anchors to bypass the negative states.

Hypnotic Anchors in Everyday Living

We can become aware of what triggers us into undesirable moments of being overwhelmed by tuning in to the feelings of discomfort and focusing on those inner feelings in trance. We need to trace the feelings back to the first time we ever felt them and see that old childhood experience with the new eyes of an adult. We can then develop within ourselves powerful stimuli that we can use to shift ourselves out of and beyond these painful moments. They are called anchors and can be used to replace old triggers.

Matthew was the fifty-five-year-old owner of a corporation who was referred to me by his doctor because of depression and the inability to sleep. When he spoke of his wife his voice changed into the high voice of a twelve-year-old child. He described listening to her and being overwhelmed by feelings of frustration and helplessness. He was consciously aware that these feelings were similar to what he had felt often in the presence of his critical and rageful mother. When he was with his wife, he had total amnesia for his effectiveness as head of a large corporation, and these feelings of impotence were beginning to affect his performance at work.

The therapeutic task was to help Matthew become aware of the state of consciousness he was in *while* he was feeling it. This is the key: stepping back from the feeling while we are feeling it, before becoming overwhelmed by it. This awareness is the first step. The second step was to help him shift into his adult, highly competent self. There are many ways to interrupt this automatic pattern.

One of these ways is to use a hypnotic anchor. Stanislavsky, a Russian acting teacher, would have his students do preliminary work with an object, associating with it a chain of feelings they wanted to evoke onstage. They would look at the object or hold it with an intensity of focused attention, which we call trance, and amplify the feeling that is connected with that object, intensely identifying with it, associating the object with the feeling. Later, onstage, they could look at the object at the appropriate time and the feeling automatically would reappear.

I decided to use an anchor that would remind Matthew of his strength and abilities. Matthew wore a ring his beloved father had given him. His father had been the mainstay of his life, encouraging and supporting him from the time he was little until he formed his own company. The ring meant a lot to Matthew and he hadn't taken it off since his father had died. Matthew already associated the ring with the feeling of strength he got from his father, so I decided Matthew should use it as an anchor. We worked with the ring in trance, and whenever he became aware of the helplessness that his wife and competitive people at work evoked in him, he would touch his ring, take a deep breath, and shift himself into his competent and decisive self. He used the ring as a trigger to remind his unconscious of his powerful and competent self so he could shift away from the downward slide of helplessness. The ring was also an anchor to help him stay connected to his good feelings about himself.

In trance he also worked with the little boy who had been so frightened by his sometimes psychotic mother, giving to that part of himself the compassion and caring that a little boy had needed when his mother hurt his feelings by her constant criticism. He used the anchor of the ring to offset the helplessness he felt in the face of the triggers of his mother's hostility and criticism.

Many years ago I had a client named Josie whose father took her with him when he visited his mistress. He left Josie sitting in the lady's kitchen. While waiting for her father, she was always aware of the lingering smell of sausage. As an adult, she often wondered why the smell of sausage excited her sexually, until she remembered all those hours sitting in that kitchen waiting for her father. This smell triggered a whole set of mixed feelings. In hypnosis she learned to separate the painful little-girl associations from her right to her own sexual feelings. She became master of an unconscious imprint by recognizing it and releasing the unwanted feelings about her father.

Remember Sandra, who was told she danced like an elephant? After remembering that painful moment in trance I asked her, "Is there another way you could think about elephants?" She then put a different frame around her picture of elephants. In trance she began to smile and wave her arms. She was having a Disneyesque fantasy of herself dancing through flowers with light-footed, graceful, and playful elephants. She anchored that image for herself by placing her thumb and forefinger together as she moved through the fantasy. Later, she started a collection of elephant figurines of all sizes and shapes. In her research she learned what wonderful and intelligent creatures they are.

And what about Susie and her struggle with the painful word "selfish"? She was able to reframe the word by hypnotically chaining and anchoring all the times being "selfish" had helped her achieve what she needed. She did this in trance by clasping her hands together every time she remembered the times she had been successfully selfish. Whenever her stomach went into spasm at the word or the thought, she would clasp her hands together and the spasm would dissolve. She turned the trigger of negative feelings into an anchor for good feelings about herself.

We are affected daily by such triggers and anchors. Many people can be suddenly irritated for no apparent reason until they become aware that a tone of voice or a certain word or phrase can reawaken some intensity that they had completely forgotten. Words and voice tones can be wonderful triggers and anchors in times of stress.

In a hospital emergency room when the emergency team is working feverishly on someone in crisis, a quiet voice speaking softly into the ear of the patient in the midst of all the noise can immediately lower blood pressure and bring reassurance to the terrorized person, who has shifted into an altered state of shock and fear. That one voice can trigger a calm state and can also serve as an anchor until the patient is stabilized. I know a nurse who, instead of saying, "Would you like your pain medication now?" will say, "Would you like your comfort medication now?" By changing the word "pain," to "comfort" the nurse triggered the patient's unconscious from the state of anticipation of pain to the anticipation of comfort. Constant repetition by the nurse consolidated that anchor. Other nurses have often asked her, "How come you get all the good patients?"

Once I received a phone call at 12:30 A.M. from a dear friend whose mother was dying of a brain tumor. "I want to help her die peacefully at home," she sobbed, "but I'm crying so hard I can't talk." When I arrived, her mother was in the hospital bed, agitated and gasping. Elaine had spoken to me of her mother, but I had not met her. She was the widowed mother of four beautiful daughters, a proud and matriarchal lady. She had loved elegant clothes, and her fondest memories, in addition to the birth of her daughters, were of dancing with her husband in Hawaii. I spoke to her gently about all her sunny and romantic memories—of the music, the breeze, the feeling of her husband dancing with her, the births and graduations and weddings of her children. Her face smoothed out, and she looked up as if she could see everything I was saying. Her face was lovely. She closed her eyes and gently stopped breathing, and then she took one more light breath and stopped breathing again—this time for good. It was a sacred moment. I think that it was the gentleness in my voice that triggered the memories anchoring her to herself and the precious moments of her life. I felt honored to be a part of that experience.

Family Rituals as Triggers and Anchors in Everyday Life

The family dinner table can be a powerful trigger and anchor. Sandy came to me for hypnosis for back pain. The doctors had told him there was no medical reason for it and he had no idea what was causing it. When we worked in trance, I asked him to go back to the first time he experienced this pain. He associated the pain with holiday times when he was a little boy. He remembered that his mother would frequently take to her bed with back pain. He was the youngest of six brothers. At the dinner table, he would try to say something and would be interrupted so often by the teasing and yelling that he finally gave up. He would sit silently staring up at the painting of a red barn opposite him. Sometimes, he would rush up to his bedroom and, like his mother, experience a terrible pain in his back. He subsequently discovered that every time he saw a red barn, his back would begin to hurt. After he moved away from home, his back pain improved—until he returned for holidays. The original negative hypnotic trigger was his identification with his mother and her way of dealing with—or not dealing with—her anger at the pressure of her family's expectations. Another negative hypnotic trigger was the picture of the red barn and all the feelings he was suppressing while looking at it. The repetition of the holiday scene anchored in his physiological response.

I think Sandy's physical pain was an expression of the emotional pain he had been unable to express, so while the original back pain went away after a period of time, he still had much therapeutic work to do to create more anchors for himself to call upon when he went home for family holidays.

Many people who have eating disorders, digestive problems, irritable bowel syndrome, or even gagging reflex problems describe the intense discomfort they chronically experienced at the family dinner table. A controlling and dominating father in whose presence children are ordered to be seen and not heard can imprint the nervous system and digestion of his more sensitive children, who then associate fear and anxiety with eating. The spontaneous satisfaction of eating when hungry and enjoying the experience of sharing a meal is cut off and the child sits, tight-lipped, nervous, and fearful, pushing his food around on his plate. Many children are forced to sit at the table until they have choked down every last unwanted bite. Often they have to learn how to relax and *then* discover the pleasure of the taste and texture of food. It is a new experience for them to enjoy something as simple as a really good home-cooked meal.

By becoming sensitive to our bodies, we can become aware of what triggers us into undesirable moments of being overwhelmed. We can develop within ourselves anchors that we can use to shift ourselves out of and beyond those moments. New anchors can replace old triggers.

Many people are programmed by their families to have a profound need to control because the family environment can be unpredictable, chaotic, covertly hostile, full of tension. Children develop coping mechanisms in order to maintain their balance in such a family; they are unconsciously terrorized by what would happen if they let go. As children they had to adopt a pattern of control in order to survive emotionally. This pattern is carried over into adulthood and often results in the inability to handle confrontation or any type of conflict. Often these patterns are passed down from one generation to the next.

Becky's father and older sister constantly fought, often coming to blows. Becky, one of seven children, was her father's favorite, and although she was terrified of his explosive anger, she developed a variety of ways to assuage him and keep him from hurting her sister.

Becky married a man who was as explosive as her father. Since the unconscious has no sense of chronological time, she continued the pattern of trying to control the arguments between her five children and her husband. She placated him and tiptoed around him, especially when he was "in one of his moods," thereby teaching her children not to express their feelings and to avoid confrontation, especially with their father. In the very effort to protect them from the terror she had felt as a child, she evoked the same fear without realizing it. Because of their courage and persistence, Becky's family is learning how to share their feelings freely. It is slow going sometimes, with two steps forward and one step backward, but the intensity of their love for each other far outweighs the patterns that have been passed down from one generation to another.

Hypnotic Rituals in Everyday Life

Family holidays or traditions repeated year after year have a hypnotic effect on family members. People will often go to the same place at the family table they sat in as children or sit in the same order year after year at church or temple. The family clown will always be funny; the parental child will always be serious; the jokes, singing, arguments will continuously repeat. Even negative patterns bring about a comfortable or not-so-comfortable familiarity. These family rituals can bring us together or tear us apart.

Religious celebrations, going to church, mosque, or temple every week, weave a design into the family tapestry that can be supporting and can enhance family life. It can also be restrictive, imprinting individual members with an intensity of experience that affects their lives continuously. In some families, adolescents will begin to rebel at the strict religious requirements to attend church, mosque, or temple, or to participate in celebrations of birthdays, Christmas, Hanukkah, Easter, New Year, graduations, bar mitzvahs, funerals.

Katie, who thought she had been "spoiled" by too much attention, was always embarrassed as a child by the lavish birthday parties her mother "surprised" her with. No matter how many times Katie asked her mother for a small birthday party for a few of her own friends, she always had to pretend to be surprised by the garden parties attended mostly by her mother's friends. Katie has always hated her birthday and, now, as an adult, is uncomfortable at any type of social gathering.

Anticipation of holidays and reactions to the aftermath take up many hours in therapy. Like Katie, many people have painful memories of family reunions in which old family feuds or disappointments are trotted out and the real purpose for the celebration is forgotten. Anxiety that the meal or party should be perfect drains the joy out of the experience and tempers flare as the first guest rings the doorbell. These associations make people "regress," or shift into the family trance when they return to the family homestead and resume their family roles. Often these people dread family reunions or holiday times. At these rituals, they experience the old familiar childhood states of consciousness as they take on their particular role in the family, sitting in the same place at the family table and often feeling invisible or unheard. They are unaware that the family ritual itself shifts them into the family trance. They find themselves saying and feeling things they had forgotten, surprising and sometimes agonizing themselves.

Brad and Liz are two young lawyers who live and work in New

York. Liz has distinguished herself in the District Attorney's office by the effective and assertive way she handles difficult cases as a prosecutor. But her authoritative, in-control demeanor vanishes when she visits her family.

"I can't recognize Liz when we go back to Illinois for a holiday," says Brad. "She becomes like a little girl. Watching her with her family is painful. She is a different person, trying to please everybody and barely talking at all, especially around her father, who is a successful attorney and head of his own firm."

Liz says, "I don't know what happens to me at these times. I become tongue-tied, I can't think clearly. I feel like I'm somebody else, or like I felt as a kid. I love my father, but, as successful as I am in New York, when I come home I feel like his sweet little princess, and I can't think of anything to say!"

One client told me: "When I go home to visit I walk in on two feet and when I leave I feel like I am crawling on all fours!"

People shift into their child roles when they return to the bosom of the family. Sitting in one's old chair at the family dinner table, looking up at the ancient chandelier or the portrait of Great-Grandmother Lucinda evokes years of emotional associations. Some say this is why there is so much alcohol consumed on these occasions. People try to anaesthetize their old, unwanted feelings. Family crises often occur in these intense moments when emotions are high and suppressed feelings come bubbling to the surface.

On a physiological level, patterns of gene expression are affected. There are hormonal changes that revivify childhood patterns of informational exchange between cells. Since the shift is on a molecular level, people relive the feelings and thoughts of their child self (say, the twelve-year-old) and in that moment forget their adult, competent self, which their twelve-year-old self doesn't yet know.

It is important to realize that family rituals shift us into automatic patterns. The therapeutic task is to recognize the triggers of the past and use the anchors of the present to avoid the shift or, if it happens, to become so self-aware that we can shift out of the family trance into a new present.

Using Hypnotic Anchors in Family Trance

Melissa, a syndicated writer for an architectural magazine, had to take an antidepressant when she became severely depressed after a visit to her family. An intelligent, articulate, and sensitive young woman who was successful in her career, she felt badly about herself and was unable to maintain a close relationship with any of the men she had been with. Highly self-critical and a perfectionist, she had always felt different from the rest of her family—especially her competitive mother. Moving away from her hometown in the Midwest didn't help her feel better.

Because she was so bright, insightful, and courageous, she did well in therapy and began to feel better about herself. Then she went home for a family holiday. She returned to New York and was in despair because she became severely depressed all over again. Hesitantly, she asked if I thought she should take medication. While I believe that medication without therapy is not particularly helpful over the long haul, I felt she needed it at the time and referred her to a psychiatrist. She improved markedly. She resumed a long-term relationship with her favorite boyfriend and felt closer to him than she had ever allowed herself to be. She became pregnant and wanted to keep the baby, so she decided to discontinue the Prozac.

What was so beautiful about Melissa was that she had learned about herself thanks to our previous therapy, plus the medication. She had been exploring her underlying assumptions about life. As a little girl, she had accepted her mother's criticisms; she believed deeply that there was something wrong with her and that she didn't deserve to have what she wanted. Using hypnosis in therapy, she had been re-framing these assumptions and began to gain a more positive sense of self. However, when she went back to the family environment for the holidays, she was inundated by all the old feelings of failure. Recognizing this backslide, and helped by the medication plus therapy, she returned to liking herself better. She was determined to maintain the good feelings she had gained about herself. The medicine had helped her feel positive about her ability to be happy. When she went off the medication, she taught herself how to use that positive feeling as an anchor to shift out of depressive thinking. "When I was on medication, I felt that it was possible for me to be happy. Off the medication, I decided to keep using the assumption that I could be happy because I experienced that it worked better for me." She had used the combination of therapy and medication well.

Melissa is now married, with three children and a thriving career. She is a wonderful example of how people can track their own process, develop awareness of shifts of consciousness, and make new connections between thoughts and feelings. When things got rocky, as they invariably do in our lives, Melissa handled the difficulties with her new self-knowledge.

Anniversary Reactions

Anniversary reactions are another trigger that shifts us into automatic behavior. Have you ever awakened and felt waves of sadness for no reason at all—until you looked at the calendar and suddenly realized it was the date of your mother's death? Sometimes we unconsciously "forget" what is painful to us.

Betsy came to me because she suddenly developed intense anxiety about her daughter, Dinah, who had just turned seven. Betsy was fearful that Dinah would do badly in school, that nobody would want to play with her, that she might be kidnapped as she walked in the neighborhood! She hovered over her daughter and even began to dislike her because Dinah, feeling smothered, began pushing her away.

When we explored Betsy's background, it came out that she had moved from Maryland to Illinois when she was seven years old. She had had difficulty in the new school, where classes were much bigger, and had trouble making friends. She would get lost in strange neighborhoods walking home by herself. In hypnosis, she remembered all of the pain and anxiety of that year when she turned seven. Now, she wanted to protect little Dinah from the pain she had experienced and forgotten.

Often clients will come in and say, "I don't know why I feel so upset today" or "I feel so happy today and I have not a clue as to what is causing this." When we explore the data and go back in time, the client often discovers an event that our feelings remember but our minds have forgotten!

Sometimes the anniversary of parental divorce or a death can trigger behavior in one member of a couple that seems to come from nowhere. In some cases, it can begin a pattern that leads to severe trouble between the couple—sometimes even to divorce. On or around this date one partner will start an affair outside of the marriage "on impulse," which turns out to be a replay of parental behavior that might have been forgotten or was never known consciously in the first place. A wife, impelled by some dark, internal fear she may not even recognize consciously, suddenly decides to go back to work or to graduate school, leaving three small children in the hands of a housekeeper. If it is a well-thought-out plan that her husband supports, and the children are well prepared and a competent housekeeper is in place, then this won't be a problem. If it is a sudden, somewhat desperate decision, it is important to look at the history of her family to determine what is motivating this action.

Often when we re-create the patterns that powerfully affected us, it has to do with unrecognized feelings or decisions, conscious or unconscious, that we made as children. When we get clear about these patterns, we get mastery over ourselves and can choose the roads that we take.

Obstacles Can Occur

Sometimes it takes courage to confront the conscious and unconscious restrictions that our experience has generated; sometimes there can be a conflict of values.

Jonathan, a doctor, referred himself for treatment because he was dissatisfied with his marriage and his work no longer was fulfilling. His marriage appeared civilized and outwardly successful. His wife, like Jonathan, avoided closeness and sex because of her own puritanical background. When he tried to persuade her to go into therapy, she refused.

Jonathan came from a Southern family with strict religious principles. He was an only child with several doting aunts and a cold, dominating mother. Jonathan's parents had a pattern of fighting loudly and then not talking to each other for long periods of time. Like many children, Jonathan thought it was his fault that they fought, and he grew up with feelings of shame and guilt. After one of the fights, his father left the family for good. Jonathan was ten and never saw his father again. Jonathan was told many times that men must be honorable and responsible, no matter what the cost; otherwise they are angry, irresponsible, and weak like his father. There was no in between. And what did this view do for him? How was his behavior affected? Did this view serve him or hurt him? Was his father really weak? Deep down little Jonathan felt that he had somehow sent his father away.

Several times out of desperation Jonathan found relationships outside the marriage that were fulfilling to him. Once he asked his wife for a divorce and she stopped talking to him for months. He felt helpless and unable to take any action. Later, he went back to the affair, rationalizing this behavior to himself because he could not bring himself to leave the structure of his marriage. Besides, his children need never know. But his wife discovered the affair. She went into rages and withdrew into icy silence. Jonathan's paralysis in response to his father's attacks and his mother's coldness was reactivated by his wife's behavior. Full of the same guilt and helplessness he had felt as a shy little boy, he dutifully returned to his loveless marriage, its predictable, well-mannered structure, and some solace from his three children.

Jonathan's religious background set great store on dutifulness and responsibility. The idea that life was to be enjoyed and that people could share their feelings was not part of the family tradition. This pressure added to his being stuck in an unsatisfying marriage. His wife's consistent refusal to go into therapy with him left him in a very difficult position. Although he wanted to find ways to break out of his childhood family constraints, he did not want to disrupt his family structure. To add even more pressure, one of his daughters had a physical disability and he did not want to leave her.

We all experience anxiety in the face of change. On unconscious levels we try to avoid the terrible feelings of the early imprints that were repressed, thinking that they would be worse than the present familiar unhappy situation. Children have no tools to protect themselves from emotional pain except amnesia or dissociation. Since the unconscious has no sense of time, it sees the imprint of a similar situation as a threat and marshals its forces against reexperiencing it. For Jonathan, the unconscious fear of experiencing the same pain he felt when his father left may have been his attempt to protect himself. He experienced the same helpless state he had as a child and was paralyzed to act—even to become more assertive with his wife.

Even though his mother was cold and distant, he felt that she was all he had after his father disappeared. His dominating mother was his pillar of strength; his "weak" father didn't love him enough to stay. Jonathan wondered whether he was weak like his father. Would he have to stay to prove that he wasn't? Jonathan lived in the same emotional environment he lived in as a child. In a sense, he was caught in a hypnotic web of fear and inaction caused by the early imprints. He had seen a number of therapists, but had not yet undergone a consistent treatment in hypnotherapy.

Hypnosis can be a powerful tool to help people deal with the anxiety of change. Sometimes in psychotherapy and hypnotherapy people can learn to come to terms with their anxiety. Medication can help, and people can learn to accept those feelings of anxiety. They can begin to realize that their present anxiety is not as terrible as what they suppressed or repressed as children, and that as adults, they have many more tools to cope with unpleasant feelings. With competent professional help they can move through the process of change and will realize that the apprehension of change can be more terrifying than the change itself.

▶ EXERCISE 9 ◀
THE FAMILY QUESTIONNAIRE

This questionnaire is to be used in conjunction with the genogram (see page 55). These are suggested questions for your exploration of the family-of-origin personalities and events. Answer the questions on your own and then ask them of your family members. If a family member is not alive or not interested, you can answer these questions as if you were that person. People who have used the questionnaire have discovered much about relationships and personalities that they only had vague ideas about. The question process itself can evoke many memories and feelings between you and the person you talk with. Family members you never knew can come alive.

Use the questionnaire in whatever way feels comfortable to you. Some people, especially older relatives, enjoy it; some people relish your sensitivity and interest. Many of my clients have tape-recorded interviews and saved them. In many cases it offers a rich experience for you and your family.

I feel this exploration is important. There is a story about a man named William, a lawyer, who had stopped talking to his father at age twenty. Forty-five years later, William got a phone call from his younger brother, Sam, saying his father was in a hospital in Florida, dying of cancer. Sam wanted William to know in case he wanted to see his father for the last time. William struggled with his ambivalence and finally made the trip to see his father.

He sat on the edge of the old man's bed and said, "Dad, I just couldn't keep trying to reach out to you. Do you know you never hugged me in my life?" His father, William Sr., said, with tears streaming down his face, "Willie, I didn't know how. Would you teach me?" The son took one of his father's skinny arms and said, "Here. You put this arm around my neck like this." Then he took the other arm and did the same. "Then you pull me close to you!" They made the connection forty-five years later. William then found out that his father's father had died when his father was three. His grandmother had had to work long hours to support him and his brother and was too exhausted to be emotionally available. "I had to fend for myself from then on," he told his son. Four days later, William Sr. died in his son's arms.

I think that if William had been able to see his father not just as the figure who disappointed him but as a human being with a whole history before he had a son, William might have been able to learn more about who his father was. He could have seen him as a whole human being. Then he would not have lost all those years and they could have really known each other.

The genogram, the exercises, and the questionnaire are designed to get you to think in wider frames about the people who may have hurt you. You may discover creative and playful ways to avoid years of estrangement and pain without giving up your autonomy and independent spirit.

Before you start, close your eyes and check your level of comfort with yourself and with your partner. Then write down the answers to the following questions. You might want to notice which ones are easy to answer and which ones are more difficult.

THE FAMILY QUESTIONNAIRE, PART I

Your Early Years

- ► Where did your family come from?
- ► Did you ever think about the towns they came from? What they might be like?
- ► Would you ever like to go back and visit them? Find your roots?
- ► What did you know/feel/learn about your grandparents?
- ► Who was (would have been) your favorite grandparent?
- ► Did you have another favorite relative?
- ► What was your relationship like with your father (stepfather)?
- ► Did you respect him?
- ► Did you love him?
- ► Did you like to be with him?
- ► What did you dislike about him?
- ► Were there ways in which you wanted to be like him?
- ► Were there ways in which you did *not* want to be like him?
- ► What was your relationship like with your mother (stepmother)?
- ► Did you respect her?
- ► Did you love her?
- ► Did you like to be with her?
- ► What did you dislike about her?
- ► Were there ways in which you wanted to be like her?

- Were there ways in which you did *not* want to be like her?
- Who were your best friends?
- What was your favorite place to be by yourself?
- What were your favorite stories? Your favorite characters in books/music/movies/theater? Did you like poetry? Songs? Nursery rhymes?
- Who was your favorite teacher?
- Whom did you love the most?
- Whom did you dislike/hate the most?
- Whose eyes did you love the most?
- Who did you want to be when you grew up?
- What were your little-boy/girl secrets/daydreams?
- How did you feel about your body as a little boy/girl? As you grew into adolescence?
- When did you have your first crush?
- When was the first time you thought you might be in love? What did it feel like?

Anniversary Reactions

- What are the important dates in your life? (Think of births; deaths; marriages; the day you got engaged, graduated, started menstruating; your first communion; bar mitzvah; starting or finishing an important project; holidays.)
- How has your selection of these dates been influenced by your mother, father, siblings, grandmother, grandfather, or by the family myths?
- What are your attitudes and memories of your birthday and others' birthdays?
- Have you ever awakened in the morning feeling significantly different—happier, sadder—and later in the day suddenly flashed onto the date and realized it was the anniversary of something? When?

▸ What dates do you always forget?

▸ What dates do you always remember?

▸ What was the happiest time when you were little?

▸ When was your happiest birthday?

▸ When was your best Christmas or Hanukkah?

▸ What was the saddest time when you were little?

▸ What were you most proud of?

▸ What were you most ashamed of?

▸ What was the most important discovery you made when you were little?

▸ What did you do on Saturdays? Sundays?

Relationships

▸ What did you think/feel the first time you met your partner?

▸ When did you decide that you really liked/loved your partner?

▸ When did you decide to be serious about your partner?

▸ What was it like the first time your parents met your partner?

▸ Did they like/dislike your partner?

▸ Did your partner like/dislike your parent(s)?

▸ What was it like when you first saw your partner's mother/father?

▸ What did s/he or they look like?

▸ How did you feel?

▸ What didn't you like about him/her/them?

▸ Was there something about your partner's mother/father that made you want to marry him/her?

▸ What were your doubts about them?

▸ What was her/his family like?

▸ How did they feel about you?

▸ How did they feel about the two of you getting together?

▸ How did your family feel about the two of you getting together?

▸ Did you love anyone before your partner? Who?

- How was that different?
- Did you love anyone after your partner? Who? How was that different?
- What were your doubts/fears about marriage?

New Arrivals

- If you have younger siblings, what did you think/how did you feel when you found out your mother was pregnant?
- How did you feel about your new brother or sister?
- How did you feel when you found out you were pregnant (or your partner was pregnant)? Did you have doubts? Were you afraid? What did you say/do? How did your mother feel?
- What were your fantasies about your first child?
- What did you think/how did you feel when the first child arrived?
- What were your first thoughts about your child?
- What did you think/how did you feel when you finally saw your child?
    as a toddler?
    as an adolescent?
    as an adult?
- What is your most cherished memory of your firstborn as a baby?
    as a toddler?
    as an adolescent?
    as an adult?
- What is your most heartwarming memory of you and your first-born together?
- What were your first thoughts about your second child?
- What did you think/how did you feel when you finally saw your second child?
- What is your most cherished memory of your second child?
    as a baby?

as a toddler?

as an adolescent?

as an adult?

► What is your most heartwarming memory of you and your second child together?

► Ask the same questions about each of your children.

► What did you like most/least about yourself as a father/mother?

► What did you learn from being a father/mother?

Your Sense of Self

► Do you remember events that marked the change from:

infant to child?

child to adolescent?

adolescent to youth?

youth to young (wo)man?

young (wo)man to mature (wo)man?

► Looking back, what did you think of yourself in those different stages?

► Which "you" do you like best/least?

► How did you discover what work you wanted to do?

► Did you have a career plan? When did you decide what you wanted to do?

► What did you like most about yourself and your work?

► What do you now like about yourself and your work?

► Did you enjoy your work before you got together with your partner?

► What do you like most/least about yourself as a husband/wife or partner?

► What do you learn from being a husband/wife or partner?

► How do you feel about yourself now?

► What is the most important thing you learned in your life?

► Who were the people who influenced you the most? What did you learn from them?

- Has your life turned out the way you expected it to be?
- What do you want to do with the rest of your life?
- What are the things you still want to do/experience?
- Where are the places you still want to go?
- Do you have a moment/memory that you recall as a resource whenever you need to feel good?
- What in your roots can contribute to helping you achieve future happiness and accomplishments?
- What in your memory can give you the tools to help you achieve those goals?

THE FAMILY QUESTIONNAIRE, PART II

Questions About the Family Physiology

Just as we absorb patterns of thinking, feeling, and learning from parents and sometimes siblings, our bodies also absorb patterns of organization and movement, which then shape our responses and choices. The following questions are designed to get you thinking about your body and your body image, and your attitude about how to care for and esteem yourself.

- Whom do you look like the most?
- In what way?
- Do you think your mother/father is physically beautiful?
    Sexually beautiful?
    Handsome?
    Ugly?
    So-so?
    Healthy?
    Well coordinated?
    Well proportioned?

▶ Does your mother/father think that s/he is:
    Physically beautiful?
    Sexually beautiful?
    Handsome?
    Ugly?
    So-so?
    Healthy?
    Well coordinated?
    Well proportioned?
▶ What is it about your mother's/father's body you like?
▶ What is it about your mother's/father's body that you dislike?
▶ How are you similar to him/her?
▶ How are you dissimilar to him/her?
▶ Do you move like him/her? In the same rhythm?
▶ Do you breathe like him/her?
▶ What is your mother's/father's attitude toward his/her:
    Face?
    Eyes?
    Body?
    Sexuality?
    Breathing?
Toward:
    Sports?
    Exercise?
    Grooming?
    Clothing?
    Self-care?
    Childbirth?
    Menstruation?
    Body functions?
    Aging?
    Eating?
    Sleeping?

▶ What are your mother's/father's physiological vulnerabilities?

▶ Are yours the same or different?

▶ When and how has your mother/father been ill?

▶ Do you think the same thing might happen to you?

▶ What is your mother's/father's biggest preoccupation about his/her body?

▶ Is yours similar or opposite or different?

▶ Do you remember what you thought about your mother's/father's body when you were little? What did you like? What didn't you like?

▶ Do you remember imitating your mother/father: the way s/he walked or pointed at you when s/he was angry? The way s/he answered the telephone? The way your mother put on makeup or perfume? The way s/he took a bath or shower? Laughed? Got hysterical?

▶ What physical habits have you learned from him/her that you have not yet been aware of?

Now answer these questions with regard to siblings and significant others (grandfather, a teacher, a family myth about someone you never met).

When you have finished, write down whatever other impressions you may have and share them with your partner if you would like.

Close your eyes for a moment and check your inner barometer for your comfort level with yourself and with your partner.

▶ Tool Kit

During the following week notice what thoughts and impressions come up about your family that may have been stimulated by the questionnaire. Notice any change in behavior that might be associated with these thoughts. Write down whatever interests you.

> ▶ **EXERCISE 10** ◀
> ## FAMILY THEMES

Go to your special place, and when you both are settled and ready, put your genogram where you can readily focus on it. Close your eyes for a moment and focus on your inner barometer to check your comfort level with yourself and with your partner.

Pick a theme you or both of you would like to transform as it relates to your partner, such as time, work, expressions of love, times of crises, loss, vacations, fun, leisure, play. Following are some examples: Sandra is always late meeting Bill; John always agrees to do certain jobs around the house and never finds the time; Sally interrupts Nathan all the time and would like to stop doing it; Jill is always tired when Sam wants to go dancing.

We will be working with money and sex in chapters nine and ten, so wait to work with those areas. Pick whatever theme comes to you (you can do this exercise anytime you want with other themes). Have your journal and a pen next to you.

Now put your thumb and forefinger together, take a deep breath, and let your breathing slowly and gently take you to your safe place. Let yourself really be there. See what you see there, feel it, touch it, taste it, smell it. When you are ready, open your eyes and think of the theme you have chosen. See if a person in your family of origin comes to mind. Think of the theme you have chosen again, close your eyes, and let your inner mind reconnect with whatever memories or associations or pictures you have of this person's attitudes, statements, or expressed feelings about the theme you picked.

See if you can recall statements they made to you or others, or behavior that you noticed, or something that left an impression on your mind. Listen to what you learned or said to yourself in reaction to those statements or behaviors. How did it affect your subsequent behavior? Does it still affect you? Is this self-statement something you want to hold on to or let go? Can you release it? What would your life be like if you didn't have this attitude in the back of your mind? Do you want to let it go? Can you let it go? When will you let it go? Picture yourself at some time in the future without this attitude. How does it feel? How do you feel when you think of it?

When you feel finished with this image, open your eyes and write down whatever you may have discovered about your own attitudes that reflects these old imprints. Notice how they have affected your choices and behavior. Have they limited you? Do they come from your own self or are they something you heard and believed as your own truth?

After you have finished, pick another person and repeat the process. Then, when you are ready, share with your partner if you wish to. You may want to do this exercise with significant figures in your genogram because different people gave you different messages. This exercise may take you several weeks. You can continue to do this exercise as you move forward in the book, or you may choose to wait until you have done all the family members before you move on.

Close your eyes for a moment and check your inner barometer for your comfort level with yourself and with your partner.

▶ Tool Kit

As you move through the week, notice what comes up for you around the theme you picked. Notice your language about it and any change in your behavior. Write down in your journal what you have noticed that you may not have been so aware of before.

5

Your Self-Talk: Hearing
What You Are Saying to Yourself
and Your Partner

The language we use is the language we learned unconsciously in our families of origin. We learn words and phrases by imitating what we hear and see. Later we make up our own language and begin to define the world around us. The infant looks up at the mother's face, hears sounds that become familiar and watches her lips shape the sounds. At one moment the infant recognizes the sound that is its very own name. As we grow, we learn new words every day and we believe what we hear because our minds haven't yet learned to prioritize or discriminate. We take in what we hear as the truth. "This is a table." Or, "You are a selfish little girl! Give Jimmy your toy!"

As we begin to separate from the mother and individuate ourselves, messages from mother are very important. Not only do the mother's messages get internalized and become the core of her child's self-identity, but ideally the mother reinforces her child's self-esteem and independence. If the mother's messages compromise the child's sense of self, he or she may grow up with the inability to trust his/her feelings and may be plagued by self-doubt. The mother's own self-distrust transfers to the child.

Sara's mother was hostile and at times psychotic. Glaring down at her little daughter, through gritted teeth she would mutter, "But I love you even if you are a bad girl." Sara could feel the hatred from her mother, but she had to choose to believe what her mother told her because she needed her mother to love her. Sara grew up feeling she was bad. This is how Sara learned not to trust her own feelings. Once, her mother told her that her Russian ancestor had put a bad spell on her. Sara believed this until she worked through it in therapy by using hypnosis, going back to those moments, seeing the scenes with her mother from her adult perspective and recognizing the truth—that her mother was projecting her own fear and self-hatred onto her daughter.

As children we tried to make sense out of disturbing experiences by talking to ourselves about them. Often with self-talk we blame ourselves for what happened or what was said to us. Taking on the blame makes a child feel less helpless; through magical thinking, a child will feel a sense of control over what happened. We may not know what we did, but for sure it was our fault! Thus we build our self-image—always trying to measure up to try to change something we didn't cause in the first place. On conscious and unconscious levels we carry this self-image into adulthood, often unaware of how it continues to affect us.

Children are forgiving. Because of their need for acceptance they will take on burdens of guilt and shame out of sheer love for a parent, even an abusive parent. Somehow the child senses that essence, that core self under all the parent's bravado or cruelty. I have seen many adults haunted by their failure to reach behind the critical or hateful persona to touch the essence of that parent. Children incorporate their failure to contact the deep self of the unreachable parent into the way they talk to themselves. "Mommy is right. I am a bad girl!" They hate themselves for being helpless and they see life as an endless struggle to win the acceptance they can never feel.

A student of mine was sent to her aunt's as a three-year-old and has spent many years working on her feelings of displacement and abandonment by her mother. There were four other children in the family. She was the littlest. Why did her mother pick her to send away?

Messages from the Past
Shape Our Future

We see life through the language we learned. "Life is a struggle." "You have to suffer to be beautiful." "When you listen to your heart you can find what you need." Whether we realize it or not, the messages we heard as children profoundly influence us as adults.

Cindy, a tennis pro, was constantly told by her mother, "Never, never let anybody get ahead of you—even running to the water cooler!" Cindy sought treatment because she had few friends and felt emotionally isolated, even though she was financially successful. She had been programmed to take from everyone, but had not the slightest idea how to give. She literally had to get lessons to learn how to transform the statement that was constantly running through her brain.

Maggie, a social worker, was constantly told by her well-meaning father from the time she was very little: "Honey, you will always be well taken care of. You will be so happy when I die because you will have plenty of money!" Maggie remembers vehemently saying to herself, "I'll *never* touch a penny of that. I don't want my father to die!" After he died she did nothing to protect her estate from greedy relatives and lived a pattern of allowing people to take advantage of her financially. Fortunately, in therapy she began to understand how her self-talk about money had caused her to abdicate control over her finances, and she proceeded to stand her ground and save what was left from further inroads.

We are constantly talking to ourselves. What we say to ourselves creates our reality. "I know I am going to flunk this exam" sets up a poor performance. "I always goof. I know I cannot ask for the raise I deserve and get it." "There is no point in trying." This language leads to what is called a self-fulfilling prophecy. What we say to ourselves leads us to make choices that make those messages come true.

How Our Self-Talk Affects Our Bodies

Becoming aware of our self-talk requires practice because we talk to ourselves on conscious and unconscious levels, often reflecting the imprints we experienced in childhood. Children take everything they hear into their bodies. An exhausted mother often repeated to her little Susie, "Running after you all the time is killing me!" And then she died. The thought that something about herself had killed her mother was so painful that Susie had put the thought of herself as a killer into the back of her mind. The feelings that thought generated were too disintegrating for a little four-year-old to process, so she mercifully forgot them. But her unconscious did not forget. Nor did her body forget. After her mother died, she suffered with chronic colitis and irritable bowel syndrome, which continued for years. The symptoms began to disappear as she worked with her forgotten feelings about herself as a murderer.

Alice had been married for twelve years and had four children. When Alice was a young girl, her mother had criticized her unmercifully and her father would say, "I am sending you to a good college to keep you out of trouble until the right man comes along to take care of you." Just as she had been told, as soon as she graduated, Alice married Jim, a college professor who taught religion. After the birth of her fourth child, Alice became depressed and dragged herself around caring for her children, barely able to move. She was diagnosed with an unspecific "liver malfunction." Because she was not being helped medically she sought psychiatric care. In psychotherapy she got in touch with years of repressed anger at her role as a passive female in the patriarchal household she grew up in. She discovered that on an unconscious level she truly believed she could never get what she needed and had covered it over with a sweet, enthusiastic persona that was almost killing her. As she became more assertive she began to like her real self better and was able to let go of all the demeaning self-criticism that had imprisoned her. Once her children were older she went to graduate school and she is now on her way to a fulfilling career in medical research. In hypnotherapy, she was able to change the conscious and unconscious conversations she had with herself, although she told me recently, "I still have to stay in tune with myself because the old voice will crop up once in a while!" Her liver malfunction has not come back in twenty years. Someone once said, "Our cells eavesdrop on our self-conversation." Alice hated herself and her body followed her instructions.

When clients get in touch with their elusive self-images, they become more aware of the hidden words they say to themselves and how those words affect their bodies.

Joseph's father always focused on his bad points . . . "for your own good." All his adult life he had been walking around surrounded by the "black cloud of his father's words," which affected his posture and his ability to breathe freely. To protect himself from his father's endless criticism, he learned early to constrict his chest muscles, which shortened his breathing. He could not feel his own feelings, only his father's. He was continuously trying to rectify his bad points. But his critical self-talk always reminded him that he didn't deserve to enjoy himself, that he had to pay for his faults. In addition to hypnotherapy, Joseph began Feldenkrais work to release the patterns in his body that triggered his mind back to the same old self-talk. Joseph is learning to like himself and to relax the muscles in his chest and back. He is learning to enjoy breathing and moving freely. There are many forms of bodywork that can increase flexibility and range of motion and give people the freedom to enjoy their bodies. Rubenfeld Synergy work is another form that combines hypnosis and bodywork in very beautiful ways to promote transformation.

When we begin to tune in to our inaudible chitchat that we learned as children we can reframe what we say to ourselves. Having the will to change can help, but willing it is not enough. Thinking positive thoughts can also help, but this kind of cognitive thinking does not go deep enough. We need to catch the elusive patterns that shift in our bodies and our minds, and reframe them in hypnosis.

For thirty yeas as a psychotherapist I have seen people begin to realize how their self-talk has run their lives and imprinted their bodies. In doing so, they connect with the image they had of themselves as children and can trace how that image has been a tangled thread in the tapestry of their lives. Remember Sally in the introduction? She saw how throughout her life she had continuously allowed herself to be beaten up to please her father. Once she saw that image, she could let go of it and move on in her life.

When clients get in touch with their elusive self-images they become more aware of the hidden words they say to themselves. Often their bodies express what they are saying to themselves. Like with Joseph, even breathing can be a clue.

People can learn to track these sensations, which often can turn into physical phenomena—headaches, stomach pains, mucus in the throat. These symptoms can express the buried words we haven't yet heard. Sometimes the words are not so buried. Just as a slip of the tongue can reveal the unconscious (as Freud said), the body words we choose to describe our feelings may tell us more when we see them as clues. Have you ever heard "Oh, she gives me a headache!" or "He is a pain in the neck!"? Our bodies hear our words and we can learn to listen to our bodies.

But how do you pay attention? You can do your own detective work. When you look at your genogram you can begin to remember moments when each of these people said something to you that you may long ago have forgotten. Pick a theme—for example, money. What did each of these people say to you about money? How did they behave? Did you pick up their unconscious attitudes? Do you unknowingly give expression to those attitudes now? Do you feel those attitudes in your body?

Ben, a multimillionaire real estate developer, sought help because, although he was successful in business, he experienced no happiness, only "flatness," which manifested as heaviness in his chest. He remembers hearing his father tell his mother that the doctor had told him to slow down or he would have a heart attack. As a child, Ben had watched his father go to work to sell fruits and vegetables at five o'clock in the morning and come home exhausted at nine o'clock at night. Now, whenever he speaks about his father, tears come into his eyes. His eight-year-old voice kept telling him, "Why can't I help him? What is wrong with me? He works too hard! He's going to die from it and I am not helping!" His inability to help his father made him feel like a failure, a feeling he carries to this day.

In hypnosis, Ben is now giving the critical part of himself permission to enjoy what he has created and not punish himself because he couldn't help his father when he was young. Now he is beginning to accept that his success is what his father was working so hard for! Now he can honor his father by enjoying his life instead of blaming himself because he couldn't help his father the way he longed to.

Elaine, a history professor, recognized in treatment how she had tied herself to her alcoholic father. As an impressionable child, when her father was verbally cruel to her she would consciously cut off her own feelings of hurt and bewilderment by saying to herself, "I know he doesn't mean to hurt me. He is really very sensitive. I am strong so I can take care of him." Elaine has been in several subtly abusive relationships. She takes care of stray dogs and cats, and when several kind and loving men came into her life she felt "smothered and unable to breathe." She couldn't accept loving behavior. She had to take care of losers because that is what love meant to her. That is how she kept her tie to the one person who meant the most to her—her abusive, charming, alcoholic father. It was only through hypnosis that Elaine was able to reconnect with the part of herself that she had cut off as a child. By allowing that little girl inside her to feel the hurt she had repressed, she was able to adjust her concept of love and was eventually able to enjoy a loving relationship with a kind and caring man.

How Words from Our Past Play Out in Our Present Relationships

We shape our relationships out of what our words convey; and our words to others are shaped by what we say to ourselves. Often we are totally unaware of our elusive self-conversation and, more important, we have little idea of how our self-talk shapes our relationships.

As adults, sometimes we hear ourselves saying to our children the very words and phrases that hurt us the most. That is because as children, when we heard painful language we relegated it to our unconscious and probably forgot the words, phrases, tones of voice, angry looks. But when we are triggered as adults by a similar situation our unconscious remembers and we relive the experience and the very words we hated hearing come bubbling up. Our internal communication system has shifted into the childhood patterns that we experi-

enced and repressed. We shift into that little-child trance and the molecular information system that occurred in that childhood experience
is duplicated.

Selma, a teacher, had a heart of gold, but could not understand
why people avoided her. She went out of her way to give to people, to
help them in whatever way she could. She was a good problem-solver
and was extremely intelligent and well meaning. When a friend told
her that she didn't want to see her anymore because everything she
said was a "put-down," Selma sought help.

Her European-born aristocratic mother criticized everything she
said and did, always with the intention of bringing up her little girl to
excel in everything. Selma's inner critic (her mother) was pervasive;
her own natural self, her own feelings had gone underground. She had
repressed her rage at her dominating mother and absent father and her
feelings of helplessness at rarely being allowed to see her grandparents,
whom she loved very much. To protect herself she had blocked out
her pain and split off the loving little-girl part of herself. She had developed a blind spot to the cruelty that hurt her so much and, in fact,
took on the aggressive style of her mother so completely that she was
absolutely unaware that her sharp tongue could cause pain in others.
She was aghast that people were upset at the way she talked to them.
Selma's heart was in the right place, but her words were disconnected
from her heart. She couldn't bear to hear them consciously.

We also take in what we hear our parents say to each other. "You
are so self-centered. I can't believe I've lived with you all these years. It
gives me a headache just to think about it!" Kitty's mother would
shout this at her husband and then take to her bed for three days with
"a splitting headache." When Kitty heard herself say something similar to her own husband she was so shocked that she immediately
sought therapy. Not only did she not want to see her husband shrink
into the woodwork after years of these onslaughts, she didn't want to
give herself chronic sinus headaches!

Have you ever said to yourself, "My God! I am sounding just like my mother!" Usually, unlike Kitty, we are so completely on automatic that we are not even aware that we are creating the same heartache we couldn't avoid as children. We are following the unconscious model we were programmed by because it surrounded us every day in what we heard and saw and felt. We began to talk to ourselves, incorporating what we heard into our own conversations with ourselves. That self-talk about relationships, money, duty, leisure, work, education, success, failure, integrity, religion—all that we took in on conscious and unconscious levels influenced our life choices.

Sylvia fell passionately in love at age sixteen and became engaged. Her fiancé went away to college, broke the engagement, and married someone else. Sylvia made up her mind at that time never to allow herself to feel passionate again. When Luke came along, he was exactly what her parents wanted for her in terms of background. He came from a good family, went to the best schools, had the proper pedigree. It wasn't until many years later, after Sylvia divorced Luke, that she found out her father had never really liked him. He found Luke cold, intellectual, and somewhat calculating. Sylvia always wondered what might have happened if her father had shared his true feelings with her. She had pursued what she thought he wanted—a civilized marriage, like his own. Sylvia's mother, who lost her own father when she was six, distrusted her husband, hated Sylvia's first fiancé, and disliked Luke. She constantly berated him to her daughter, who lived out her mother's suggestions and eventually divorced Luke. Sylvia internalized the messages she received from her parents and eventually made them her own. In turn, those messages dictated what she did in her life.

Alicia, a stepmother, was obsessively jealous of her husband's thirty-four-year-old daughter whose financial and emotional demands threatened her to the point of saying to her husband such things as "You love Dominique more than you love me!" Alicia's alcoholic father had been enabled by her mother, who devoted all her attention to this passive and troubled man. As a child, Alicia had felt that her mother loved her father more than she loved her. Alicia perceived that she was back in the same pain she had lived in as a child. In turn, her demands on her new husband were beginning to drive him away until they sought treatment together.

Messages about love and marriage from our past can have a powerful effect on our present relationships. In moments of tension we hear ourselves repeat what our parents said to each other and which we took in unconsciously: "Mother was right. Men never do what you ask!" "You always interrupt me, especially when I am about to make a point!" "I have sacrificed myself all these years for you and what thanks do I get?" "You never listen to me. I feel like I am talking to a brick wall." And the ultimate hypnotic suggestion: "I know you don't love me." Said in a tone of voice that is harsh and angry, these are toxic statements that can poison a relationship.

We can learn to tune in to the unconscious destructive flow of messages we live by *before* we communicate them to our partner and can stop these messages from the past from damaging our lives today.

► EXERCISE 11 ◄
FAMILY MESSAGES IN HOW WE TALK TO OURSELVES

Go to your special place and sit quietly for a few moments. Close your eyes and check the level of your comfort with yourself and with your partner. Just notice.

Put your genogram and your family questionnaire in front of you. Take a pad of paper and a pen and write down the following themes, each on its own page.

- Work
- Education

- Religion
- Spirituality
- Fun
- Community
- Politics
- Gender
- Time together—Relationships

Focus on each theme for a while by closing your eyes and exploring your thoughts, memories, assumptions, and beliefs about that theme. Notice what comes up in terms of what you say to yourself. What did you hear other people say? What did you observe about their attitudes? Write down what you have discovered. See if you can pinpoint how other people's beliefs and language have influenced your own.

Do this for each theme.

After you have finished, review what you have written and see if you can find a common denominator that characterizes each of them. Do they form a foundation for possibilities and growth? Do they limit your horizons with regard to yourself, your abilities, and what you would like to achieve in your life?

Close your eyes and imagine yourself in a room with blackboards on all sides, with what you have written on your pad up on those blackboards, each theme by itself in its own panel. Imagine erasing each one until there is nothing written on any of the blackboards except the themes. Then go around the room and write in each panel what beliefs and assumptions you would like to have for each of those themes.

Then sit in the middle of the room and look all around at what you have written, as if you were in a museum looking at and learning from great works of art.

When you have finished, leave the room, open your eyes, and write down whatever comes to you.

If you wish, share whatever happened and whatever you have learned with your partner.

Close your eyes for a moment and check your comfort level with yourself and with your partner.

▶ Tool Kit

Look at the list of themes several times during the week and notice any new associations that come up in your mind. Notice any changes in your behavior, especially in any of these areas. Note them in your journal and let your mind keep percolating.

▶ **EXERCISE 12** ◀
HOW YOUR SELF-TALK
CHOREOGRAPHS YOUR DANCE
WITH YOUR PARTNER

Go to your special place and sit quietly, looking at your partner. Close your eyes for a moment and check your inner barometer for your comfort level with yourself and with your partner.

Put your notes from the previous exercise in front of you along with your pad of blank paper. Again write down the same themes, each on one sheet of paper.

If you are working with a partner, write down your impressions of how you think your family-of-origin programming has choreographed how you have communicated with your partner in relation to these themes. Take enough time to let your unconscious help you make new connections as you write down what you are discovering with regard to each theme.

If you are doing this exercise alone, take each theme and notice how your family-of-origin programming has choreographed your attitudes, feelings, and behaviors in each of these areas.

When you have finished, close your eyes, put your thumb and forefinger together, take a deep breath, and go to your safe place. When you are there with all your senses and your feeling of comfort, security, and serenity, put a screen up in the front of or in the back of your mind. Let an image form of you and your partner exploring these areas together. Notice any changes in what you are saying or doing.

When you are finished, open your eyes and write down whatever comes to you. If you would like, share it with your partner.

Close your eyes again for a moment and check your inner barometer for your level of comfort with yourself and with your partner.

► Tool Kit

During the week notice any new associations or connections you are making regarding how your self-talk choreographs your communication with your partner. Write down what you have discovered.

6

The Iceberg: What You See Is Not What You Get

Freud discovered the unconscious, Milton Erickson talked with the unconscious, and Virginia Satir drew a model of the unconscious that can help people identify the shifts from conscious to unconscious states. She called it "the Personal Iceberg of Unexpressed Inner Life." Our observable behavior is the tip of the iceberg. Under the surface are many levels of years of intense feelings, reactions, and decisions that we have lived through.

See page 110 for the iceberg model. Following is a description of the levels that affect our emotional and physical development:

Behavior

This is the level of conscious, observable behavior. It is the action we take to achieve something, to follow the story line of our lives. It is also the reactions we have to what happens to us.

Coping Stances

Satir described four ways that people defend against feeling the wounds they have sustained. She called these "the crippled communication stances." I have added a fifth—the withholder.

The *blamer* projects inner feelings of humiliation, shame, or guilt that he cannot face onto other people. "It's all your fault."

The *placater* represses all his own feelings in order not to lose approval or love. "I'll do whatever you want. Just don't leave me."

The *computer* has turned off all feelings and filters experience through a dry intellect. "This situation has reached a level of unfathomability and I surmise that the best way to handle it is to talk rationally."

The *distracter* uses confusion not to feel anything. "Have you seen *Jaws 2*? Oh look, you have a spot on your tie!"

The *withholder* represses feelings out of fear of loss of control and refuses to communicate.

We all move from one of these stances to another. In times of stress we usually fall back on one stance that we may have learned from a family member.

"Congruent communication" is when we can freely match our words with our feelings.

Feelings and Feelings About Feelings

There are feelings that drive behavior. More important, there are feelings about the feelings. When we are angry at ourselves for what we feel or criticize ourselves for what we feel, we amplify the feelings even more. Letting go of the feelings about the feelings makes it possible to observe the feelings and explore the roots. Acceptance of the validity of our feelings is important because then we can more easily track the mistaken perceptions that may cause them.

Anger often masks other feelings that are harder for us to allow ourselves to experience or look at—anxiety, fear, shame, humiliation. Going beneath the anger often enables us to really understand what is going on. We will explore anger more thoroughly in chapter eight.

Perceptions, Beliefs, Assumptions, Mind-Set

When a child has an experience and there is deep feeling, an imprint happens. The child will often talk to himself to make sense out of what he perceives. Sometimes the child's mind is not yet able to see the whole picture, so a mistaken belief about the experience occurs and is often relegated to the unconscious. The perception occurs out of unmet expectations.

Expectations

Children are born with the expectation that their needs will be fulfilled. Sooner or later their expectations will not be met. When parents try to please the child at all times they create deeper frustration in the child later on. The wise and sensitive parent will accept the child's frustrated feelings and gently maintain the boundary so that the child feels understood even though the limits are maintained. Parents are not perfect; sooner or later the child will face frustration.

The Need for Love, Universal Yearning

Studies have shown that infants who are not touched and loved will languish and die. We all need to love and be loved. When the child does not feel accepted he will feel unworthy of love and create belief systems that will search for evidence that he cannot find love out in the world.

The Core Self, Essence, Life Force

The self is separate from the yearning for love, the expectations, the beliefs, the feelings, the behaviors. This is the most vulnerable, creative, and powerful part of each of us. Some people call it soul. This is what Erickson called "the unconscious," and you can tap into it through self-hypnosis, meditation, prayer. When you develop a relationship with this part of yourself, you can master all the other levels that you operate from. This core self is at the bottom of the iceberg. Some people sense it in their heart, some in their solar plexus, some in their "gut," some say "all over my body." It is a knowing that is not logical or rational.

When we follow the iceberg in the lessons at the end of this chapter we can discover new roads to the sacred and vulnerable parts of ourselves—many of which have remained hidden to us. There are memory treasures that we may have buried long ago along with precious parts of ourselves. We can rediscover these sacred parts by using the map of the iceberg to go on our own inner journey.

Before the practice lessons, which you can embark on together or separately, we will see how two couples used the iceberg model and how it helped them break through the barriers that kept them from getting closer.

Sandra, a nurse, sought treatment because she was severely depressed. She had begun to hate having sex with her husband, Charlie. She even changed her hospital schedule to avoid him at night.

When we explored her childhood, Sandra acknowledged that she had adored and feared her father. He was a kind man, except when he drank. At those unpredictable times he would suddenly and unex-

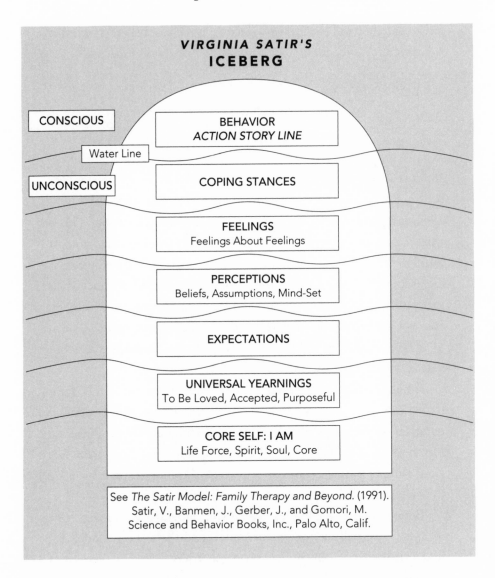

VIRGINIA SATIR'S
ICEBERG

CONSCIOUS

BEHAVIOR
ACTION STORY LINE

Water Line

UNCONSCIOUS

COPING STANCES

FEELINGS
Feelings About Feelings

PERCEPTIONS
Beliefs, Assumptions, Mind-Set

EXPECTATIONS

UNIVERSAL YEARNINGS
To Be Loved, Accepted, Purposeful

CORE SELF: I AM
Life Force, Spirit, Soul, Core

See *The Satir Model: Family Therapy and Beyond.* (1991).
Satir, V., Banmen, J., Gerber, J., and Gomori, M.
Science and Behavior Books, Inc., Palo Alto, Calif.

pectedly hit her, so she never knew whether he would slap her or touch her gently. This came out in a session when I asked her if she knew why a little muscle on her left cheek under her eye would twitch whenever she mentioned her father. She also discovered that she was afraid of Charlie, although he had never hit her. Sometimes he was funny and the next minute he became rough. His big hands hurt her when he held her. She reflected, "He is like my father. One minute he is funny and warm and the next minute he is scary."

Sandra had suppressed most of her feelings and had been "the perfect child." Her mother was "a saint," who expected Sandra to follow closely in her footsteps, and Sandra did. She escaped into her studies and spent a lot of time in her room, lost in fantasy. She was a brilliant student and is now supervisor of a special research project at a prestigious university hospital.

Charlie, a big and gruff high-school football coach, loves Sandra deeply, but was becoming more and more angry at her coldness. He resented her withholding and felt that she used her depression to punish him. He had six brothers, and his father, like Sandra's, was alcoholic. His family consciousness was laced with seething violence and brutal wit. Charlie had had to fight for every bit of attention he got and when that didn't work he played the family clown.

Sandra and Charlie were very bright people who had adopted two children and then had twins of their own. They respected each other, had been good friends, and had worked well together with their children.

When they implemented the iceberg model, they discovered how profoundly their difficulties had been programmed in their original families.

To describe how this couple used the levels in the iceberg model I will list the level and quote each partner.

Sandra:

Behavior: "My rejection of Charlie is terrible, but I can't stand for him to touch me! It has been building up in me for a long time. Once, I even read the paper while he had sex with me. I had to distract myself!"

Stances: "For years I was a placater. I did whatever he wanted because I was so afraid he would stop loving me. I felt so bad about myself. Sometimes I drank a lot of gin at night just to numb myself. But I got so depressed, went into therapy, and discovered how angry I was. Then I became a blamer. That is when I moved out of the bedroom."

Feelings: "I am so angry at him because he keeps blaming me! He blames me for being depressed. Then he blames me for being withholding. I know it's my fault, but I just can't do it anymore. And I am tired of the criticism! I hate myself for being such a drag. I hate what I feel."

Perceptions and beliefs: "What is behind my self-loathing is the belief that no matter how hard I try, I am just not good enough. Deep down I am a terrible person. What generates that belief? The assumption is that if I were any good, Father would never have hit me so much. There must be something really bad in me that he was punishing me for all the time."

Expectations: "I guess I expected Father to be kind and loving to me all the time. I think I tried to trust him, but after a while I was afraid of his hitting and my whole body would freeze and get numb. I think I gave up wanting him to love me. I didn't stop loving him, but I now realize I also began to hate him."

Need for love: "Do I have a right to love? I never thought of it that way. When he wasn't drunk, my father was more loving than my mother, who was very cold. I wasn't really loved by either of them, or at least I couldn't feel it, so I guess I gave up the thought that anybody could love me. I started to pretend to be as good as I could so that people would love me anyway and leave me alone. But I couldn't really feel good about them or myself."

The core self (the part that has the need for love): "I don't think I trust the part of me that is what you call my core self. Perhaps it's my soul, which I have always prayed for but never sensed.

"Do I have the right to be angry? Yes, I think so, but I am afraid to show it. And I shut down when Charlie gets angry, which is most of the time."

By using this model, Sandra got down to her core self. She discovered that she could love that deep-down part of herself that had tried so hard and persisted with her work in spite of so many buried feelings. At my suggestion, she found photographs of the little girl she had been and studied them. She wrote letters to little Sandra before she went to bed. She also stopped drinking so much gin. As she developed a genuine compassion for the little girl who expected to be loved and got hit instead, she learned to let her feelings flow. She cried a lot, wrote a lot, and gradually got in touch with the lively little Sandra who had been sitting in the back of her mind in the dark, thinking that no one would bring light to her! She discovered that she had a bubbly and witty sense of humor, a part of her that never had had a chance to express itself.

Charlie's story was different:

Behavior: "I like being aggressive! I think it is important for me to be as aggressive as I am because otherwise I won't get anything. And I like being good at being a clown. I have a great sense of humor! I can distract people that way and get what I want! They laugh at me but it doesn't bother me."

Stances: "I have to believe that everyone else is wrong so I fight for what I need, so I guess I am a blamer. When that doesn't work I become a distracter. I am good at that, too."

Feelings: "I am angry most of the time. I hate being angry all the time, but I don't know how else to act."

Perceptions and beliefs: "The belief under that is that I won't get what I need unless I fight for it or make jokes about it! I can't be a softy! Not where I come from! Dad beat us all up and the best day of my life was when I knocked down my oldest brother, Jimmy, the family bully. And when I couldn't fight, I could make jokes and still get what I needed!

"I guess I always felt that I wouldn't make it in life if I didn't use my fists and my wits. Sissies were losers. My working assumption was that life is a jungle and that I could pretend to be powerful and funny and get away with it."

Expectations: "What expectations? I gave up having expectations the day Jimmy got the bike I had wanted for three years. That was always the way, and Mom never helped. She was too weak!"

Need for love: "Sure I have a right to it. I need Sandra to love me, and she used to, or so I thought. Now it's like living in an armed camp! I tried to be aggressive, to show her how much I loved her; I tried to be funny. Nothing worked."

The core self: "I know that part of me needs love and sex and it is angry as hell. But the anger doesn't help either. Nothing works, and now I am getting as depressed as she used to be."

When they began to realize that under all the rage and potential violence there were other unexpressed feelings, they began to experience each other differently.

In one session, Charlie was expressing his sadness and grief that he no longer felt desired by Sandra, that when he approached her she turned cold. I asked him to show me how he communicated his need for her. He jumped up with his big hands spread wide and lunged toward Sandra, clutching both of her arms tightly.

Sandra suddenly froze, her eyes dilating and her body stiffening. A little muscle on her cheekbone began to twitch. She stared up at him and gasped, "I just can't!"

Charlie threw up his hands, looked at the ceiling, turned ashen, and stared helplessly at me. We explored his feelings at that moment and he admitted that underneath the assertiveness was profound anxiety and the fear that he would be rejected again. Sandra said, "But you frighten me when you look like that!"

Then began the lessons in touching, gentleness, becoming aware of the subtle changes in facial expression, color. After they felt safer, they practiced pretending to be animals: Sandra wanted him to be a big, soft white rabbit, or a gentle mother lion or a sensitive, kindly deer. Charlie wanted her to be a playful, laughing otter, a beautiful Persian cat, a baby lamb that he could hold and take care of.

Later, when I asked them to have a nasty argument as one of the animals and pantomime the action, the once-bitter argument became hilarious and we all had a good laugh! In those moments, they each connected to the core in the other.

As time went on, Charlie's innate gentleness and good-hearted sensitivity began to emerge—especially in the way he touched Sandra. Tenderness replaced anxiety and unconscious anger. Her depression evaporated. She developed a healthy, lusty ability to have sex with him. Sandra stopped working nights.

The iceberg helped them to step back so each could recognize in the other the interplay of feelings and fear that they had orchestrated from childhood until they got to the trembling, naked core vulnerability that is the best and most human part in all of us.

Every time they practiced they learned to interrupt the painful patterns they evoked in each other. In the ensuing silence, playfulness, warmth, and loving filled the empty spaces.

Something new was added and the old patterns could no longer hold their power! New energy flowed.

Every couple develops its unique variation on the theme of the couple's trance. Constanza, a writer and illustrator of children's books, came from a noisy, volatile Italian family. She was the fifth of six children and was beaten up and molested by her next older brother when she was four years old. Constanza's father was explosive and her mother was alternately dominating, hypercritical, and emotionally unavailable.

115

She sought treatment because she had periodic outbursts of explosive anger and felt out of control. She wanted to get pregnant, but was concerned about her relationship with Friedrich, her husband of three years.

Friedrich was a soft-spoken, German aristocrat. When he was two, his father went to South America, leaving Friedrich's mother alone to raise her son. Friedrich's mother was aristocratic and had many lovers, often traveling abroad without him, leaving him at home with a series of nannies. Friedrich never saw his father again. He attended British schools, went to Oxford, and came to this country to become an international banker. Extremely narcissistic and very beautiful, Friedrich's mother held her son on a very tight rein and was supercritical of Constanza's spontaneity and brilliance, competing every moment with her daughter-in-law.

When we worked with the iceberg model, here is what Constanza said:

Behavior: "I get so frustrated at Friedrich's rigidity, I don't know what I am saying. The more he looks at me blankly and shuts his mouth, the more rageful I get. I just want to throw something at him! He is so silently righteous! He one-ups me with his superciliousness and I just can't take it!"

Stances: "I used to be a placater or a distracter just to please him. Now I am a major-league blamer."

Feelings: "My feelings of rage are out of control and I don't know what to do with myself. My God! If I had a baby what would happen?

"I hate myself for feeling this way! Sometimes I hate that I still love him."

Perceptions and beliefs: "The belief behind this is that I am invisible! No matter what I do or say I am not seen and I am not heard. The more helpless and tinier I feel, the more I feel that Friedrich doesn't love me. He just stands there quietly. I'll always feel alone like I did as a kid!"

Expectations: "My longing for love went unfulfilled and I felt that nobody loved me no matter how hard I tried or how mad I got! I felt like screaming in the dark! Sometimes I would lock myself in the bathroom when nobody was home and scream into a pillow."

Need for love: "That is the story of my life. I guess I never give up because I keep fighting for it even though it never works. I don't know what else to do! The part of me that needs love? A babe crying in the wilderness! Where in my body? In my heart I guess. A big ache in my heart—or in my gut."

The core self: "The part that has the hurt? That's me. I can't be me without the hurt. What do you mean? I am separate from the hurt? I can take care of the hurt? There is a part of me that can handle the hurt? I don't think so!"

Constanza took a deep breath and explored her need for love. She had always felt unlovable and ached for love in her heart. We separated the part of her that was the love in her heart—her very essence—from the part of her that needed to love and be loved. She began to realize that her core self was not the need for love because it already knew what love was. She was able to step back and have compassion for little Constanza. Under the longing and sadness was a fierce little fighter!

Friedrich's perceptions of what was happening between them were totally different.

Behavior: "I freeze when Constanza starts criticizing me. She tells me that I am unfeeling and always have to be right. Most of the time I feel that I really am right! She is constantly erupting and I close down to protect myself from the storms of words. Also to bring in some balance! My mother was so distant. She just laid down the rules and never raised her voice."

Stances: "I guess I turn into a computer that has crashed. I feel numb."

Feelings: "I just want to escape and go to my business. I don't like that I have to be so stern with her. I don't like the way I act sometimes, or the things I say, but she brings it on."

Perceptions and beliefs: "I truly believe I am right most of the time. I also believe that I have to stay in control. She certainly can't. The underlying assumption for that feeling and that behavior? If I don't stay calm and collected then everything will blow up and disintegrate."

Expectations: "When I was a boy I never had a father and I turned to my religion. I learned through prayer to find strength. Anger is not love. It is not peaceful and it leads to a loss of control. I tried to teach myself not to get angry. Just walk out of the room. But she comes after me, screaming!"

Need for love: "My need for love is very real—but not for aggravation!"

The core self: "The part of me that is different from my need for love is my soul, which is sacred and which I have to protect! I can't let her rage and anger poison me!"

Constanza and Friedrich have a passionate relationship. When I first worked with them there were some stormy times. Constanza would see me regularly for several months at a time and Friedrich would attend infrequently.

Constanza worked a lot on her verbal and nonverbal language—how to convey how she felt with authenticity and feeling without having to go ballistic, which was her family's style of communicating. The softer she became the more Friedrich responded.

I think that Friedrich began to realize that underneath all the layers of fire and rage was a passionate, loving, intense little girl who was not made of stone and who couldn't destroy him. The irony in the situation is that he probably married her because she gave full expression to what he had never been allowed to do or feel.

As they each got in touch with how their different backgrounds and styles of feeling had caused their mutual pain, they were able to relax with each other and work together, remembering that underneath the behavior was a whole other world of feeling and perception.

▶ EXERCISE 13 ◀
WORKING WITH THE ICEBERG

Sit quietly listening to your breathing, being aware of the silence. Close your eyes for a moment and check your inner barometer for the level of comfort you have with yourself and with your partner.

Turn to the iceberg model on page 110 and each of you draw a copy of the iceberg in your journal. Don't worry if you're not an artist; all you need is to make sure you represent each level of the model. Each time you write down the description of the level, notice what you are thinking. Save these sheets for subsequent exercises in this chapter and in chapter seven.

When you are both ready, set the timer for twenty minutes. Close your eyes, put your thumb and forefinger together, take a deep breath, and go to your safe place, breathing in the sights, sounds, and smell of it, getting in touch with a sense of peace that may become more and more familiar to you when you let your thumb and forefinger come together as a signal to let go into a sense of comfort.

Now think of a behavior of yours that you would like to understand better or transform. See yourself in the situation, hear yourself talking, or perhaps become more aware of the feeling. Then pick up your pen and write down whatever comes to your mind. Is there a particular part of you that behaves this way in certain situations? Has this part of you always been there, or has it emerged just recently? Does this behavior fit into the category of stances that I described? If so, which one or ones? Write it down without thinking too much. Just let it flow onto the paper.

Notice what you are feeling. Is it an old, familiar feeling? Where does the feeling come from? Is it different from the behaving part of you? As you begin to notice the feeling, does it become stronger or less intense? Write down what is happening at this moment and where in your body you feel it.

Now how do you feel about what you feel? This feeling may be entirely different—a different part of you. Does it remind you of anyone or something someone said to you? Is it someone else's voice? Do you like it?

Now what is the belief you have about that feeling? Is it an assumption you made about life or about people or a particular person a long time ago? Did it come out of an experience that was really intense—a shock, a loss, a rejection, or a statement that you didn't understand and tried to make sense of by telling yourself this belief? Is this a belief you have about a lot of your experiences, a number of your choices? Is this belief a truth you feel about your relationship to life, to the universe? Is it a major theme of your life on some level? Does it lie at the root of much of your behavior and personality? What exactly do you say to yourself?

Take a look at what is underneath that belief. Do you remember when you formulated it? Did it come from unfulfilled expectations? Was there a time when a part of you expected something to happen with all your heart and it never did happen? Is this at the root of your feelings and beliefs about yourself and the world? Write down whatever comes to mind.

Do you think that the unfulfilled expectations come from your own need for love, your need to be heard, your need to connect on a heart level? Is that part of you still there and still waiting to be fulfilled? Are there moments when you feel this connection with your heart? When are they? Is this a part of yourself that you can experience fully?

Write down whatever comes to mind, the first thing. It may surprise, shock, or delight you. It may not.

Now close your eyes and take a deep breath. See if you can go beyond that part of you that needs to be loved. This part is not the needy part, or the feeling part. It is separate. It is the part of you that is your core self—that is beyond the need or the feeling or the belief or the behavior. It is who you are apart from any one of these experiences. Some people call it your soul, your higher self, your core self. Whatever it is called, it is *you*—without a sense of time or place, without words, and it experiences your unique knowing.

It is this part of you that is at the root, the foundation of the iceberg. Just be with that and then write down whatever comes to mind.

When you have completed this lesson, sit back, take a deep breath, and take as long as you want in the time that you have left to come back to the room. If you need more time, set the timer again for a new agreed-upon time. Then when you have finished, share your thoughts with your partner if you want to, or just let them percolate. You may notice some new thoughts or memories coming up in the days following this exercise.

Close your eyes for a moment and check your inner barometer for your comfort level with yourself and with your partner.

▶ Tool Kit

During the next week you may notice more clearly not only what you feel, but also what you feel about that feeling. Make a note of it. See if you can trace the underlying belief that is at the root of that feeling, or even at the root of the unfulfilled expectation. Just notice. Also, pay attention to any changes in your behavior and write down whatever seems important to you.

> ► **EXERCISE 14** ◄
> WORKING WITH THE ICEBERG
> WITH YOUR PARTNER

Get a batch of 8½-by-11-inch blank sheets of white paper or a pad of paper and two markers.

Let yourself get comfortable in your special place and, as you listen to your breathing, become aware of how gentle it can be and how comfortable you can feel just letting yourself be.

Close your eyes for a moment and check your inner barometer for your level of comfort with yourself and with your partner. Look at the model of the iceberg on page 110. Each of you take eight pieces of paper and write down each level on a separate page. The first paper will say "Behavior." Each of you should have one page representing each level. However, make two pages for "Feelings": one for "Feelings," one for "Feelings About Feelings." Place your papers in a vertical line on the floor in front of you. You and your partner's line should be parallel, with the two sheets marked "Behavior" at the top, facing each other.

Now, together choose a topic that you disagree about. Since this is the first time you are working with the iceberg model, pick something that isn't too serious, something that each of you, or one of you, is uncomfortable with about your partner's behavior or your own. Maybe you experience some conflict because one of you always seems to control the remote control and decides what to watch on television. Or maybe you have an issue about leaving the dishes in the sink. It can be anything. Just trust what you come up with. Make sure you both agree that this is the right topic for now. When you have agreed, each of you step on your "Behavior" sheet.

Remember, this is not a matter of who is right and who is wrong. This is an exercise in saying exactly what is true for you, no more, no less.

A and *B* stand facing each other. *A*, begins and *B* repeats exactly what *A* says, refraining from commenting or disagreeing, but noticing what feelings come up.

Here is an example:

The person with the lightest hair, *A*, goes first and says: "I say that when I [behavior] want to change the channel you never [behavior] even hear me." *B*, who has the darker hair, repeats: "When you say that you [behavior] want to change the channel I never [behavior] even hear you."

Then *A* steps onto the next sheet, marked "Stances," and says: "I think that when I become a placater [stance] and give in you become a withholder [stance] and ignore me."

B then steps onto the "Stances" sheet and says: "When you think you become a placater [stance] and give in, I become a withholder [stance] and I ignore you."

Then *A* steps onto *A*'s sheet marked "Feelings" and says: "When this happens I feel angry and constricted in my stomach."

B steps next onto *B*'s sheet marked "Feelings" and says: "When this happens you feel angry and constricted in your stomach."

A steps onto the next sheet marked "Feelings About Feelings" and says: "When I feel this I feel mad at myself and I get a pain in my stomach about my feelings."

B steps onto the sheet marked "Feelings About Feelings" and says: "When you feel this feeling you feel mad at yourself and you get a pain in your stomach about your feelings."

A then steps onto the sheet marked "Perceptions" and says: "When I feel mad at myself I believe I shouldn't have these feelings."

B then steps onto the sheet marked "Perceptions" and says: "When you feel mad at yourself you believe you shouldn't have these feelings."

A then steps onto the sheet marked "Expectations" and says: "When my expectations are not fulfilled I just assume I'm wrong and don't deserve to have my way."

B then steps onto the sheet marked "Expectations" and says:

"When your expectations are not fulfilled you just assume you are wrong and don't deserve to have your way."

A then steps onto the sheet marked "Need for Love" and says: "When I need to be loved I feel sad that it doesn't happen."

B then steps on the next sheet and says: "When you need to be loved you feel sad that it doesn't happen."

A then steps onto the sheet marked "Core Self" and says: "When I get in touch with my core self that has all these behaviors, feelings, assumptions, expectations, and yearnings I feel compassion for that part of me and want to express it more."

B then says: "When you feel in touch with your core self that has all these behaviors, feelings, assumptions, expectations, and yearnings you feel compassion for that part of you and want to express it more."

Now you have read the sample together. Pick a theme and follow the outline, going from one level to the next.

When you have finished this part of the exercise both of you write down whatever your impressions are and then, if you wish, share them with your partner.

If you are doing the iceberg with your partner, shift and run through the exercise again with *B* speaking and *A* listening.

If you are doing this exercise alone, you can have one chair for *A* and one chair for *B* and move back and forth from one chair to the other as you move through the exercise. As you do it, notice how you feel in each chair and if there is a shift in your awareness.

After you have finished the whole sequence and have written down your impressions and shared them, close your eyes for a moment and check your inner barometer for your level of comfort with yourself and with your partner.

▶ Tool Kit

Continue to notice the levels that you shift to in your discussions, arguments, or interchanges with people, especially the people you care about. Write down whatever you find important or whatever may make you curious.

> ▶ **EXERCISE 15** ◀
> ## WORKING WITH THE ICEBERG WITH
> ## YOUR PARTNER—A VARIATION

In your special place sit quietly and notice how comfortable you feel, almost as if it is an anchor for you to get in touch with yourself.

Close your eyes and check your inner barometer for your level of comfort with yourself and with your partner.

When you are both ready, take your iceberg sheets of paper and again lay them on the floor. Now that you are familiar with the exercise, you may get a little more creative. Think of something else that the two of you disagree about or have feelings about. And then, when you have agreed on a topic, pick an *A* and a *B*, *A* having the lightest hair. This time *B* can go first.

Do the exercise as you did it before, but this time add a part of the self that reacts.

For example:

Stepping on *B*'s sheet labeled "Behavior," *B* says: "When I say I would like to talk, you ignore me and change the subject. There is a part of me that wants to grab you and shake you to get your attention."

Here is your model:

Stepping onto the sheet labeled "Behavior," *B* says: "When I do or say_____you always do or say_____. There is a part of me that_____."

A steps onto the "Behavior" sheet and says: "When you do or say_____you say I always do or say_____. There is a part of you that_____."

Stepping onto the sheet labeled "Stances," *B* says: "When I become a_____and_____, you become a_____and_____. There is a part of me that_____. Etc."

Continue the exercise through to the end. When you say, "There is a part of me that_____," notice this part of you. Can you locate it in your body? Is it a victim ("This part of me just wants to give up. My whole body is tired.")? A placater ("This part of me just gives in because I don't want a fight. My sciatica is killing me.")? A blamer ("This part of me gets frustrated because you are so selfish that it keeps our marriage a mess. I've got a migraine coming.")? A lonely part ("Part of me feels more alone than if I was single. I feel tears behind my eyes all the time.")? A distracter ("Part of me doesn't like fixing dinner. My stomach hurts. You look hungry. Let's go out to eat.")? A compartmentalizer ("Part of me probably gets upset, but I don't feel it.")? A withholder ("Part of me shuts down. I will not talk to you right now.")? A wild part ("Part of me is just itching to run away from this marriage, get a motorcycle, and take to the highway.")? Just notice these parts of yourself as they come up and watch how your body responds.

When you have finished, close your eyes, put your thumb and forefinger together, take a deep breath, and go to your safe place and just be with yourself. Then, when you are ready, write down whatever comes to you. If you want to, share with your partner.

Close your eyes for a moment and check your inner barometer for your comfort level with yourself and with your partner.

If you are doing this exercise alone you can, as you did in the first exercise, become more aware of parts of yourself. Put part *A* in one chair and part *B* in a facing chair and switch back and forth.

Notice any changes as you move back and forth. Then close your eyes and check your inner barometer for your comfort level with yourself.

▶ Tool Kit

Continue to notice how you shift in your communications with people and with yourself. Are you becoming more attuned to that deeper level, that more vulnerable part of yourself? Are you aware of any changes in your behavior? Write down what you notice.

▶ **EXERCISE 16** ◀

USING THE ICEBERG TO TRANSFORM A BEHAVIOR OF YOUR OWN

Put your thumb and forefinger together, take a deep breath, go to your safe place, and really enjoy letting go of whatever burdens you came in with. Close your eyes and check your inner barometer for your level of comfort with yourself and with your partner.

Look at your sketch of your iceberg. As you are looking at it, think of some behavior of yours that you would like to transform, something you do or say or feel or think that you are not so comfortable with. Then just look at the iceberg and let your mind move from one level to the next, seeing yourself doing the behavior, then noticing the feeling, then the feeling about the feeling, and just continue, noticing what comes up for you. If and when you reach that vulnerable core part of you, just embrace it and be with it—kind of like taking your own vulnerable self into your own heart, as if you were being a parent to yourself. Then when you are ready, write down whatever may be important to you and bring your attention back to the room.

Close your eyes and check your inner barometer for your level of comfort with yourself and with your partner.

▶ Tool Kit

If and when anything comes up in the week that is not so comfortable for you, take a few moments to take a deep breath, and maybe, if it is appropriate, close your eyes and run through the iceberg and just notice what may happen.

▶ EXERCISE 17 ◀
USING THE ICEBERG
TO TRANSFORM A BEHAVIOR
CONNECTED TO ONE OF YOUR THEMES

Go to your special place and take a minute to get present in that space. Put the model of the iceberg in front of you. Close your eyes and check your inner barometer for your level of comfort with yourself and with your partner.

When you are ready, let your thumb and forefinger come together, take a deep breath, count to five, and then as you let go of the breathing, let go of the tension in your body. Become more and more aware that each time you focus on a tense part in your body and breathe into it, you are giving it permission to let go and find its perfect balance, its perfect rhythm, which you can become more and more attuned to and enjoy.

Open your eyes and think of a behavior that is related to one of the themes you have been working with in your genogram that you would like to explore. Then access the feeling this behavior expresses. Connect with your feeling about the feeling. What is your belief about this? Did it come from some unfulfilled expectation or some misperception, yours or another's? Was there a need for love under that? And what did you tell yourself about it? What was that part of you that did the talking trying to say?

When you have finished, write in your journal whatever you have discovered, even if it makes no sense to you.

Close your eyes and check your inner barometer for your level of comfort with yourself and with your partner. Just notice these.

▶ Tool Kit

Notice during the week whatever thoughts come to you that reflect or resonate with some part of this exercise. Notice any changes in your behavior. Write them in your journal.

Reclaiming Your Ugly Duckling:
You Are More Than the Sum
of Your Parts

We are complex beings. Each one of us has many parts. Often they are conflicting. There might be some parts we are not even aware of. Some of the parts of ourselves are our child part, our adult part, our loving part, our angry part, our professional or business part, our creative part, our humorous part, our sexual part, our spiritual part, our sad part, our guilty part, our mourning part, our show-off part, our rebel part—and many others that are uniquely our own. We are constantly moving and shifting from one part into another—or, to put it differently, we are shifting from one state of consciousness into another.

Remember in the introduction when Sally shifted into her four-year-old self and got in touch with the boxing scene with her brother and father? Sally shifted into that part of herself because she went into trance when Don yelled at her. At the same time she was aware that she was an adult, sitting in my office. She literally was in both places at once in her experience of herself. That is why she was able to shift out of the need to placate a father figure. Intellectually, she knew that she had always been afraid of her father's displeasure, but it was not until she allowed herself to experience that fear that she could dissolve the pattern on a cellular level.

In another case, a client I will call Jeanie got in touch with two different parts of herself that she experienced at different times in her life. She was able to choose the part she wanted to access more frequently and amplify it to use in her present predicament.

Jeanie was a sensitive, somewhat shy young woman who came for hypnosis to help herself become more assertive and enthusiastic, and to leave an unfulfilling job. In hypnosis she got in touch with a memory, the intensity of which had imprinted her. When she was five her mother had scolded her. Humiliated and angry, Jeanie got her dresses out of the closet and an extra pair of shoes and was climbing down the stairs, carrying the dresses on little hangers over her shoulder. Her mother confronted her at the landing: "What are you doing?" "I'm mad at you and I'm leaving home!" little Jeanie screamed. And then it came: Her mother said, "Where will you go?" Suddenly the reality of her helplessness overwhelmed Jeanie. She couldn't run away from home *or* from her feelings. A kind of paralyzing numbness overwhelmed her as she climbed back up the stairs dragging her dresses behind her. She repeatedly had this feeling of paralysis when she wanted to do something new, like leave her job. This imprint had affected her powerfully.

She discovered an earlier memory that she wanted to use as an anchor. "I had been a lively and adventurous three-year-old," she said. She used to play with a chow and a spitz who lived across the street. She didn't remember it, but the family story was that she opened the gate on her grandmother's porch and went out into the world on an adventure. She was found walking through an empty field of tall grass holding on to the collar of each of the dogs. "I was fearless at this age," she said, and it was this memory that she amplified to use as an anchor for moving into unfamiliar places. She reconnected with the spunky little girl, and hypnosis brought her through her years of surrendering, reframing many of the moments that the paralyzing imprint of nowhere to escape to had influenced. Jeanie had discovered the part of herself she had longed for and was able to use it to get a job that she could enjoy.

Jimmy and his wife, Bertie, came for couples counseling because Bertie was threatening to leave him. "His apathy and passivity are driving me crazy!" Whenever she would ask him to do something, he would sit and stare at her "almost as if he was in trance—you know, like a rabbit that is caught by the headlights of a car."

Jimmy owned his own small manufacturing company and was effective at work and with his employees. He had a few friends, but very little outside interests. Bertie was a vice president of a public relations firm, very fast-thinking and fast-moving.

Jimmy, an only child, described two different parts of himself. Up until he was ten years old, when his father died suddenly, he had been president of his class, captain of his baseball team, and he had many friends and was very outgoing and fun-loving. He had a warm relationship with his father; his mother was cold and apathetic. She became more depressed after the death of her husband.

The other part Jimmy described was a "loner" part. After his father died, he took to his room, paid little attention to sports, dropped his friends, and studied a lot. He felt that the funny, fun-loving Jimmy had died when his father died. There was no one else in his life that he cared about until he met Bertie. She had a lot of energy and he let her take charge of the marriage. After their first child was born he felt "left out" and retreated even more into himself.

Jimmy is still working on retrieving the energy that went underground when his father died. On some level, Jimmy is still mourning the loss of the one person with whom he had bonded so completely. He buried himself in work just as he buried himself in his studies.

There are many people who have a mourning part in themselves, often in reaction to the death of someone they deeply love. It is almost as if the inner mind is protecting the self from having to experience the intensity of that feeling again. This is not unlike the way Abraham's mind was protecting him from going back to war by holding on to the headache for twenty-five years. This is not a conscious process, and often people need to work with it in hypnosis to recognize how powerful it is. It can be complicated.

Many years ago I had a client whose alcoholic husband drank himself to death, leaving her with six children to raise. Ten years later she came for help in mourning him. She had been so angry following his death that she would not let herself cry, and for ten years she stoically held on to all that grief. She had put many parts of herself into a dark corner in the back of her mind. It is important that we invite these parts of ourselves into our whole personalities. This means we develop compassion for those parts of ourselves.

Many people hate or fear those parts of themselves. There is a small group of people who have reason to fear parts of themselves because they were so viciously abused as children that the parts of themselves cannot recognize each other. There is an amnesiac barrier between one part and another. These people can be helped by skilled professionals. If you think this might apply to you, please see the appendix at the back of this book so you can find out what you need to know to help yourself.

When I ask a client, "How do you feel about the child that you were?" I often hear, "I can't stand that little child. I was a nerd, helpless, stupid." Those are only a few of the adjectives people use to describe their child self. Inevitably, these people are treating themselves exactly as the toxic parent treated them. It is as if they identify with the aggressive parent against the helpless child. This can happen for years, without the person's conscious knowledge.

Kevin, a thirty-four-year-old computer consultant, came into treatment because he had painful and torturous relationships with women. Kevin is the oldest of three sons. When Kevin was three, his mother became ill and spent many hours in a darkened room, away from her children. She died when Kevin was seven. His father came into the kitchen and told him that his mother had died, and he remembered running out into the snowy night behind the garage and making a vow that he would never cry.

His father was a brilliant but at times psychotic individual who became emotionally dependent on his oldest son as his wife became more seriously ill. Having been dependent on his wife, he turned to Kevin to take care of him emotionally, telephoning him three or four times a day and demanding that Kevin spend more time with him. Kevin had a difficult time holding his own with his father and suffered terrible guilt.

Shortly after his wife's death, Kevin's father married a narcissistic woman who was overtly seductive with Kevin, especially when he was in his teens. As far as he can remember she did not sexually abuse him, although she "came close to it." She would criticize his father behind his back and after eight years she divorced him, maintaining unpredictable connections with her stepson.

At thirty-four, Kevin hated himself for being a "wimp" like his father. He hated his stepmother for being so manipulative. The only good memory he came up with about his mother was lying in her arms as an infant, feeling warm and content and loving the smell of her.

His pattern with women was to seduce them intensely until they fell in love with him and then pick fights with them and eventually drop them because they were "manipulative" and he couldn't trust them. He would leave them before they left him.

Kevin first had to learn how to accept and love the feisty, proud, arrogant little boy he had been and then become the father to himself that his own father could not be. He used hypnosis to shift himself out of the anxiety states he would move into when he became close to a woman, and access the tough little seven-year-old. He began to recognize that the anger he felt was really anxiety, and to stop the pattern, he had to take a deep breath and step back from the situation. Slowly, Kevin began to trust himself. He learned how to trust his own unconscious. He accepted that his anxiety was valid; the hurt little boy who had lost his mother never wanted to feel that pain again. When he felt himself becoming close to a woman, he was able to recognize that, even if he lost her, he now had more resources in himself to cope with the loss. He could take care of the helplessness that had overwhelmed him as a child. He saw that he was different from his father and would not become helplessly dependent on women.

We all struggle with broken dreams, loss, rejection, and feelings of inadequacy because we were children once. Children are open to life and all it brings before they learn how to protect themselves from the inevitability of disappointment, no matter how effective and loving the parents can be. We all experienced disappointment in childhood and invariably the emotions attached to those disappointments are carried into adulthood. Erickson said that there are two certain things in life—change and suffering—and that our job is to bring as much joy into life as we can. That joy is the experience of connection with the inner self, a connection that is not dependent on outer circumstances and yet is related to everything in life. This inner connection is characterized by "not doing" anything but by "being." We lose the connection when we "try," "make an effort," criticize ourselves, or judge others. Our critical part has its own value, but it is separate from the special part of the mind that I am referring to. We each have a part of ourselves that has an integrity all its own. People call it by different names: soul, higher self, chi, life energy, the god within, flow or playing in the zone. Whatever you want to call this part of yourself, learning how to recognize it, connect with it, and honor it is what I think psychotherapy is all about. I think it is what coming alive is about.

This "inner connection" propels us into relationship, with ourselves, with others, with the world. It is active, creative, and has the energy of movement in it. Moshe Feldenkrais, an Israeli physicist and Judo master who worked hypnotically with the mind-body, said, "All life is process; movement is process; change the quality of the movement and you change life itself." Becoming attuned to your inner movement is what this connection is all about.

Your inner movement is the part you connect with when you go into trance. People can connect with it in meditation, in prayer, in contemplating a beautiful day, in playing or listening to music, in singing, in creating or becoming absorbed in a work of art, in doing something they love, or in making love. They can connect with it in moments of closeness to each other. Do you remember when you felt an opening within you, looking into the eyes of someone or hearing a passage of music? I think a great artist is in touch with this part of himself so intimately that he projects it into his work, and it is that connection that we respond to. Mozart said that his favorite way of composing was to take a walk through a garden, enjoying the beauty, and suddenly, in one moment a whole symphony would come to him and he would go inside and write it down. Perhaps that is why Mozart's music touches us on deep levels. Mozart trusted his creative self and the doors of his mind opened for all of us.

Trusting this part of yourself requires a special awareness that you can develop. This part of our mind is not perfect; it came out of our childhood perceptions, which are often distorted. The act of self-acceptance, or self-forgiveness, opens the doors of self-trust. You can do this by inviting your self-critic to spend ten minutes a day doing what it knows how to do best—criticize you. (There is an exercise you can follow at the end of this chapter.) It is important that you honor the self-critic before it can relax a little and enjoy life. It has been working awfully hard to motivate you to become perfect, which we all know is not humanly possible. But this part of your mind doesn't know that because when you were little, it set up its rules in order to get what it thought you needed. Even though it is many years later, it still keeps trying, like poor Abraham and his twenty-five-year headache.

In the state of consciousness that Erickson called trance, lying to oneself just doesn't work. On this level we know when we are lying and the free flow of our energy stops. Trusting the self, trusting your unconscious, only happens in the pure state of your own truth when you move into your inner rhythm with yourself.

Have you ever been with someone who is inwardly peaceful and clear-eyed about the world and its difficulties? They are so at home with themselves that they open up the space around them for other people to be more centered and self-trusting. They live in a world of laughter, absurdity, and wisdom and they honor the creative life. These people have learned to trust the inner part of themselves.

When a couple embarks on a voyage of self-discovery, each person has to come to trust his or her own unique inner mind. Each person has his or her own road. In that sense it is a lone journey, although you can share your experiences together. On this lone journey you come to know your own self better and that can strengthen and enrich you. You then have more of yourself to share with your partner. You may fear that by doing it alone you will become too separate from your partner. However, I think you will find pleasure and freedom in two unique individuals enjoying their coming together, rather than two people who have lapsed into one automatic pattern after another with no differentiation between them.

I believe your relationship with the inner part of yourself is as sacred as your breathing, which keeps you alive each time your lungs contract and expand. Your connection with your inner self is similar. It is like the air we breathe. When you experience it you become reenergized and renourished. It is as if a part of you were a musician that is playing your music every day, except, like your breathing, you are not particularly conscious of it. Then one day you begin to hear your own music, which has been playing all along, and it sounds pretty darn good. This is what working with hypnosis and trance can be about.

▶ EXERCISE 18 ◀
YOUR SELF-CRITIC

This exercise requires only fifteen minutes. Let yourself get comfortable, and set the timer for fifteen minutes. Check your inner barometer for your level of comfort with yourself and with your partner.

Let your thumb and forefinger come together and let your eyes close. Take a deep breath and hold it for the count of five. When your breath releases, let yourself move into a state of comfort and pleasure. Go to your safe place and then invite in that part of yourself that is always criticizing you and discounting what you are doing or who you are.

Take a good look at this part of yourself. How old is it? What is it wearing and what does it look like? Ask it what it needs by criticizing you.

Then thank it for trying in its own way to help and ask it to criticize you for fifteen minutes so that you can truly understand what it is trying to do.

When the timer rings, thank this part and then come back to your comfortable place and open your eyes. Write down whatever you noticed, and then, if you like, share with your partner.

▶ Tool Kit

During the following week do this exercise by yourself for fifteen minutes at least three times, more if you think you need it and can schedule the time. Notice the changes that are occurring and write them down.

▶ EXERCISE 19 ◀
BOARD OF DIRECTORS MEETING OF THE PARTS OF YOURSELF

The following exercise will use the parts of yourself that you have come to know through your work with the genogram and the iceberg. These are the parts that have identified with parental or family figures, have taken on their words, phrases, ways of being. They are also parts of yourself that express themselves through your self-talk (i.e., the critic, the perfectionist, the downer, the one who has to be right or have the last word, the placater, the blamer, the lover, the distracter, the computer, the withholder, the innocent child, the wise one, the angry one, etc.).

Write down as many parts of yourself as you would like to have at this particular board meeting. You may want to give them names or the names of the people you have identified them with.

When you are both ready, set the timer for twenty minutes, close your eyes, put your thumb and forefinger together, take a deep breath, and go to your safe place. Notice how your senses are becoming even more sensitive and intense, how you can enjoy shifting yourself into this safe inner space of yours.

Then construct in your mind your special conference room. It can be a room that has everything that you love in it, no expense spared. It is your very own design and gives you pleasure just to think about it. You may want to continue to change it as you practice this exercise, or maybe you want to add new things that you enjoy as you go along.

Then, with your eyes closed, invite each of those parts of yourself into your board room. You can seat them as you like or have them sit wherever they want. Bring the meeting to order and put on the table some issue that you would like to explore with them. You may want to ask questions or sit back and see what these parts of you have to say. Just let your mind play with this. There is no right way, only your way. Take as long as you need in the time you have set for yourself.

When your meeting is finished, set another meeting time if you want and adjourn. Write in your journal whatever comes up for you, and then, if you want to, share with your partner.

▶ Tool Kit

During the week notice how you are shifting from one part of yourself into another. Then notice any changes in how you are thinking or communicating. Do the parts communicate differently? Write down whatever comes up.

▶ EXERCISE 20 ◀
LISTENING TO YOUR BOARD
OF DIRECTORS

Go to your special place. When you are settled, set your timer for twenty minutes and put your journal, your genogram, and your model of the iceberg in front of you. Check your inner barometer for your level of comfort with yourself and with your partner.

Let your thumb and forefinger come together, and let your eyes close. Take a deep breath and hold it for the count of five. When your breath releases, let your whole self move into a state of pleasurable comfort. When you are ready, open your eyes and think of some recent communication you have had with your partner that you would like to present to your board.

Then close your eyes and go to your safe place. When you are completely comfortable with yourself, invite your board members into your conference room. Let them be seated and then bring the meeting to order and present to them the issue about communication with your partner that you would like to discuss. If you are doing this lesson without a partner, just think of a communication problem that you would like to explore.

Sit back and observe the meeting, or you may want to ask specific questions to specific parts. Have fun doing this lesson and getting to know more about the parts of yourself.

When you have finished, come back to your special room, write down whatever you bring with you from your board meeting, and then share with your partner whatever you would like, paying attention that you each get equal time.

Check your inner barometer for your level of comfort with yourself and with your partner.

▶ Tool Kit

During the week notice when you are aware of any changes in how you are communicating with your partner. Is it from a different part of yourself? Jot down in your journal anything you may notice.

▶ EXERCISE 21 ◀
BOARD OF DIRECTORS: COMMUNICATING WITH YOUR PARTNER

If you and your partner by chance picked the same issue in exercise twenty, repeat exercise nineteen, each going to your own board about the issue. Then communicate about the particular issue with each other, being aware of how you shift from one part of yourself to another.

If you and your partner picked separate issues in exercise twenty, then work on both issues alternately. The issue of the person with the longest hair goes first. Working with your board of directors, each of you put this issue on the table and notice how the parts of you are reacting. Then when you come back to each other, commu-

nicate about that specific issue. Repeat the exercise with the other partner's issue.

▶ Tool Kit

Notice during the week any changes in how you are communicating. What part of yourself do they come from? Is your behavior
changing?

Your Angry Part: Fighting the Wrong Battle

We all carry around an angry part in ourselves because we were all children once and we all had unfulfilled expectations. This anger can be expressed and dissipated. It can be suppressed or repressed, which causes constriction in our bodies, our feelings, and sometimes our thinking. Or it can be consciously recognized and withheld. Anger not put into words can cripple our relationships.

As you explored parts of yourself in the previous chapters you may have been surprised by an angry part you didn't know you had. This is because you probably learned to suppress or repress your anger early on. In some families, anger is not allowed; in other families, only the parents have the right to express their anger and the children are neither seen nor heard. Parents who were beaten or violated as children and who repressed their anger at the abuse tend to repeat those patterns with their own children. The anger comes up from deep within them and is transmitted from one generation to another, often on unconscious levels.

Remember Sally, whose doting father watched while her little brother boxed with her until she cried? In hypnosis, Sally became aware of the unconscious anger she had felt toward her father, even as she tried to please him. From those beatings on, she had repressed her anger, even through three abusive marriages. When she remembered the boxing scene, she got in touch with her anger and was able to honor it as a healthy part of herself. But she had spent all those years bottling up that rage, unable to express her true feelings. As a child she had split off the angry part of herself and sent it underground because she so desperately wanted her father's approval. As an adult she could honor the little girl she had been and accept the unwanted anger that had kept her imprisoned. In doing so, she freed herself.

Because unspoken anger usually comes from the core part of ourselves that has been hurt, it can seek expression when we fall in love. When we fall in love, the most vulnerable part of ourselves becomes involved and our unfulfilled longings come to the surface. Susie said, "I don't understand it. No one has ever been able to push my buttons like John can, and I love him so much!" John says, "I don't get it. She is always mad at me and explodes at the smallest things!" When John forgets to do something Susie thinks is important, like picking up the laundry on his way home, Susie feels it as a rejection, reminiscent of her father's neglect of her mother. When John lost his job, she nagged him every day no matter how many headhunters he had contacted. Susie saw in him her father, who could never adequately support his family. The repressed anger at her father came bubbling up, and John became its target.

People who have been programmed not to accept their anger tend to project it onto others. It is too painful for them to admit, much less accept. To protect themselves from the recognition of the pain they are in, they blame others. Those closest to them and those they can reveal themselves to usually become the focus of their anger.

Often people don't know or cannot remember why they are so angry. But if the anger can be recognized, acknowledged, and accepted, it can be dissipated and will no longer have the power to sabotage relationships. This is not to say that anger will no longer be a part of our lives. There is plenty to be angry at in this world. Anger is part of our everyday living. But we can get creative about it instead of letting it run our lives. There are ways to channel our everyday anger that can transform relationships rather than demolish them. Once you are aware of your anger, can accept it and express it in words, or painting, or music, or dance, or golf, or tennis, or running, you can master it and stop it from messing up what is most important to you.

Learning how to shift out of the angry part of ourselves may be the most important thing you can learn in this book. The inner barometer can be your tool. You can train yourself to pay attention to the changes in your feelings and to immediately recognize the triggers that cause you to go ballistic, saying and doing things you wish you hadn't.

Repressed anger is often hard to recognize. Antonio said, "I go numb when someone confronts me. It is like a switch goes off in my head and I feel nothing and can say nothing. Sooner or later I try to figure out a way around the problem, or how to get out of it quietly." Antonio's father had used sarcasm and dismissal as a way to erode his son's self-confidence. It wasn't until Antonio started using the same behavior toward his wife that he became aware that he had learned this from his father as a way of protecting himself from his own anger. As he became more in touch with his anger he said, "My anger is so great that I am afraid that if I get in touch with it I will really hurt someone." Gradually he learned in hypnosis how to get his anger under conscious control, to accept it and express it appropriately.

Some people do not repress anger so much as withhold it. I had a student who, at age forty, began to sob when she described how her mother would get angry at her and not speak to her for two or three weeks at a time. That is a devastating experience for a little girl whose mother is the most important person in her life.

Withholding anger can kill a relationship. It can drain the life energy out of any communication and leave it dry and limp on the floor. "When he gets like that," Estelle told me, "tight-lipped and with a blank look on his face, I feel numb inside and I have no place to go and hide." Not talking keeps the anger going, keeps the couple stuck. Withholding is the real joy-killer. Often people withhold because they, like Antonio, are afraid of what will happen if they express it.

Some people feel great relief when they learn to express their anger. Sometimes they can hurt their partner, and the relationship, by inappropriate expressions of anger. We sometimes spin into these states, escalate, and hear ourselves say or yell words we later regret. So it is important not only to recognize your anger when you start to feel it, but also to learn how to say it in words so that your partner can hear it, words that serve to strengthen the relationship, not break it down.

The first step is to become aware of your anger, especially if you have had to repress it all these years. "It wasn't until I could pinpoint where my anger was in my body that I learned how to control it, to shift out of that internal space, step back, and take some time before I said anything," Ted said.

When your body feels restricted, when your breathing is short, when you look at yourself in the mirror and see those lines in your forehead, shoulders hunched as if protecting the chest, jaw tight, you may recognize someone whose body is signaling that it is holding in powerful energy. Some people will say, "It is like a knife in my chest." Others can identify it as "tightness in my throat" or "a knot in my stomach." You can take a deep breath, and as you relax notice what you are feeling. Some people are afraid to relax too much for fear of the feelings underneath, so take it at your own speed, gradually becoming familiar with the comfort you can generate just by letting yourself relax.

The second step is to accept your anger. This is difficult for people who have been brought up to fear it or deny it. Your angry part is a precious and powerful part of yourself. Usually it is the part that has suffered the most pain. Often the first time people accept their right to have their angry feelings they burst into tears, saying between gasps of air, "I feel so angry and sad and sorry for that little child who had to feel that terrible pain." And that is the beginning of their compassion for themselves—and their acceptance of their own anger.

Like Antonio, many people have bottled up their anger for so long that they are afraid if they start to communicate they will really explode and hurt the relationship even more. This is a realistic fear. If you think this is true of you, give yourself permission to work with your anger a step at a time. Patience and practice can pay off because you are in the process of changing an old, probably well-entrenched pattern. Becoming explosive all the time may be a temporary relief, but it doesn't work. Discharging feelings that have built up over time at the expense of the partner's feelings is not communication.

The process of accepting your right to feel sadness and compassion for your angry part can shift you into a state of confidence and clarity in what you want to say. Saying that you feel really angry but are having a hard time putting it into words and need more time to process it can be a gigantic first step. "I feel" can be two magic words, especially if the usual way was to blame the other person for causing the problem. Sometimes writing your anger out on a piece of paper or in a letter that you don't send can help you get control over the anger and the hurt.

The third step is to speak your feelings so clearly that what you are saying will be communicated to the other person. When you speak the truth from your heart, your ability to accept your own anger without blame or guilt will open the door for the other person to hear you. Saying what you feel shows respect for your partner and shows recognition that he or she will be able to deal with what you are sharing.

▶ EXERCISE 22 ◀
MIRROR, MIRROR ON THE WALL

Go to your safe place and put a mirror in front of you. When you are comfortable, think of a time when you were really angry and focus on that feeling. You may close your eyes and picture what happened, noticing your breathing and the feelings in your body. Then when you are ready, pick up the mirror. Notice your forehead, eyes, jaw. Notice your shoulders and chest and pay attention to your breathing. Then sit down again and let your thumb and forefinger come together, take a deep breath, and go to your safe place, letting all your senses take it in, seeing the sky, the trees, the sunset, breathing in the fragrant air, feeling comfort, relaxation, and energy flowing through you. When you are ready, pick up the mirror again and study your face and your body. Do you see a difference in your eyes? in your jaw? in your shoulders?

Now, in your mind's eye, go back to the scene of anger. Notice if it has changed. Pick up the mirror and look at your face.

Then go back to your safe place, put your thumb and forefinger together, and notice what you feel.

Repeat this sequence several times until you can become aware of how easy it can be to shift from one state to another.

Write down whatever comes to mind. Check your inner barometer for your level of comfort with yourself and with your partner.

Share with your partner whatever you would like.

▶ Tool Kit

During the following week, when you notice you are getting angry, put your thumb and forefinger together and go to your safe place. In this way you are moving away from the scene. When you come back a minute or two later, notice if there is a difference in the way you feel. Do you have more control over what you say or don't say? Write it down in your journal.

▶ EXERCISE 23 ◀
ACCEPTING THE ANGER AND BYPASSING THE CONFLICT

Let yourself get comfortable. Put your thumb and forefinger together, take a deep breath, go to your safe place, and think about exercise twenty-two—the mirror exercise you just did. Go over it in your mind.

Then when you both are ready, think of something that makes you angry. If you are doing this alone you can do it with parts of yourself that are in conflict.

A goes first and describes what makes him or her angry. *B* listens. *A* puts thumb and forefinger together, shifts into his or her safe place, breathes it in, and then says something in addition. *B* listens.

Here is an example:

A says: "I was so angry when I got home late last night and the dishes were all in the sink when you had promised to do them after your dinner!" *B* listens.

A puts thumb and forefinger together, takes a deep breath, goes to her safe comfortable place, and when she comes back she says: "I know you may be tired, too, and you may have had something else to do, but I really appreciate it when you do what you say you're going to do. Keeping your word means a lot to me."

B says: "I understand that you are angry and that you feel the way you do. I feel angry that even when I am tired you expect me to keep the whole house in good order. Everything has to be so neat all the time."

B then puts his thumb and forefinger together, takes a deep breath, goes to his safe place, and when he is ready to come back, he says: "However, I also appreciate that you are such a great housekeeper and I enjoy having everything in its place."

By going to their safe places, *A* and *B* were able to step back from their immediate anger, which they accepted by stating it, and widen their perspectives. In this way, the truth is told and the incipient conflict is bypassed. Both partners have a right to their own feelings, and when they each can accept that fact their relationship can deepen.

If you do this exercise and the anger is still there, go through the sequence again and let yourself go deeply into your safe space. Notice what changes occur with the shifts back and forth.

▶ Tool Kit

As you go through the week, notice that it can become easier to shift away from the anger just by putting your thumb and forefinger together, taking a deep breath, and going for a moment to your safe place. Write in your journal whatever comes up for you.

▶ EXERCISE 24 ◀
USING THE ICEBERG WITH
A SPECIFIC ANGER

Get yourself comfortable and put the model of the iceberg in front of you. Think of a specific time when you were angry and visualize the scene. Then put your thumb and forefinger together, take a deep breath, and go to your safe place, breathing in the comfort. Then open your eyes and, using the model of the iceberg, move through each level, noticing what is coming up for you. Somewhere in there you may be able to find the root imprint that has fed your anger.

When you have finished, write in your journal whatever you wish and share with your partner if you would like to.

Check your inner barometer for your comfort level with yourself and with your partner.

▶ Tool Kit

When you feel anger coming on during the week, think about the levels in the iceberg and notice what comes up for you. Check your inner barometer before and after. Write in your journal whatever you notice.

9

Money Myths:
Getting Money Differences
Out of the Way

How couples handle their finances can be a major and chronic irritation to each of them. It is often rooted in the attitudes they absorbed from their families of origin. These attitudes can also be harmful to the individual who holds them because they generalize and affect every aspect of our lives. Money symbolizes how much we give, how much we take, and how much we withhold.

Jennifer is a very generous person; her husband, Fred, is parsimonious by nature. Their differences in attitude affect everything they do and every decision they make. When divorce does occur, all the frustration on both sides gets focused on money issues, and the results can be very painful for everyone concerned—especially the children, who may have been aware of their parents' differences for years. Many of our attitudes toward money come from early imprints.

Money Imprints and How They Can Affect Us

Do you remember my client Maggie, from chapter five, whose father told her she would be happy when he died because she would be well taken care of? Maggie allowed her first husband and several friends to exploit her until she discovered in hypnosis that she had wanted no part of her father's money because she "associated it with his death."

Maggie worked with the iceberg exploring her self-statement about money. The behavior pattern she saw was that she virtually gave her money away by not letting herself see the manipulations of greedy people and never saying "no." The feeling she had was fear and anxiety. She had so much anxiety that she went blank whenever she thought about money. Her belief was "I don't want to have anything to do with money!" The unfulfilled expectation was that if she didn't think about it, her father wouldn't die. But he did die and then some part of her mind denied it—denied her hatred and avoidance of money.

When she explored it, she realized that she had associated her father's death with having money, and because she loved him she turned away from money altogether. She saw how her survival mind couldn't stand the thought of his death, and how she had blocked on the whole subject of money. But she also recognized for the first time something about her father's love—how deeply he loved her and wanted to protect and take care of her, even after his death. Once she saw things clearly, she was able to let go of her little-girl hatred of money and hold on to the recognition of how much her father loved her. She freed herself and is now enjoying making money on her own and saying no when appropriate. She can also now say yes with a full heart.

At the root of Maggie's money issues was her perception of her father's message. Another child might have heard this same statement differently. That child might have heard the caring part of the statement and blocked out the reference to his dying. Or if Maggie had heard it when she was a little older, she might have grasped what he meant differently. As she explored her father's background she found clues as to why she may have internalized her father's words the way she did. Her father was the oldest and brightest of four children and had taken responsibility for his siblings and his own three children. He may have communicated indirect resentment of all his responsibility, which Maggie may have been aware of unconsciously.

In this family detective work, it is important to work with the genogram and the iceberg to see the whole picture. Life is not simple and the more levels we can see the more compassion we can develop for ourselves and therefore for others.

Money and Women

Many women who come from patriarchal families have an emotional blind spot about money because the message they received was that they are incompetent in the area of finance and they are to be taken care of first by their fathers and then by their husbands. Some women were sent to college "to keep them out of trouble until the right man comes along." The women's movement has made inroads on this attitude, but the unconscious undercurrents are still there. They manifest in the phenomenon of the glass ceiling, and many women still feel inadequate when it comes to finances and handling money.

Iris was brought up by a doting father who treated her like a little princess as long as she did what he wanted. She learned early not to express her independent spirit. Iris's mother had been brought up in poverty. She saved every penny, spent little on herself or her family, and resented the lavishness that her husband bestowed on their only child. Iris had graduated from a women's college cum laude with a degree in French literature, but had no intention of working. She told me ruefully that she had been brought up to major in shopping. She married a Harvard-educated congregational minister who came from a puritan New England background and was as frugal as Iris's mother.

Her husband, Benjamin, held the purse strings and doled out small amounts of money to Iris every week. She was miserable. Because she had been brought up expecting to be taken care of by a loving and generous husband, she felt imprisoned, especially after her first child came. They could afford help, but Benjamin refused, saying it was important for a mother to be with her child at all times, as his mother, also the wife of a congregational minister, had been. Iris had been brought up by a father who treated her lovingly, as long as she "behaved." She was programmed to please her father and she continued that pattern with her husband, so she went along with his wishes.

Iris grew extremely depressed and began to hate her husband, her life, and even her child. She knew she needed help and wanted to seek counseling, but without any money at her disposal, she felt trapped. She wouldn't turn to her father to pay for therapy because he was ill. Her mother, always "in the woodwork," would be no help. Finally, her husband grudgingly paid for her treatment because he was concerned about her health, although he refused to participate with her.

In hypnotherapy Iris was able to shift from the little-girl part of herself that so badly needed her father's approval to the adult woman who was able to stand on her own two feet with Benjamin. As she worked on her ability to articulate her own needs, she reconnected with her love of French literature. When her father died she could afford to hire a housekeeper and enrolled herself in graduate school.

Benjamin was able to see the difference in Iris and eventually was able to accept her earning her Ph.D. and supported her working part-time as her two children were growing up.

These two people had been programmed differently in terms of their expectations of each other. Iris struggled to break out of her unhappiness. It took a lot of courage for her to grow up, and I think it was the love for her father and for her husband that sustained her through some difficult times.

Money and the Family Trance

If money is a bone of contention in a family, the children grow up with their unique variations of blind spots about money. When there is much pain, the cause of the pain goes underground to emerge later. Often people will use money the way others use food or alcohol—to comfort or soothe themselves or to numb the pain. Credit cards and credit card advertising do not help these people, and this can wreak havoc in a marriage if it is not dealt with. This negative hypnosis is in our culture and can have a crippling effect on people who are struggling to get by and raise their families with integrity and decency. For the people who have grown up with the experience that money or not having money causes pain, the messages from our current culture can cause trouble.

Matthew had been brought up as a playboy. His father was self-made and wanted his son to have everything that he didn't have as a boy. Matthew, who is extremely bright, sailed through college and law school barely opening a book and started his own firm. When his father went bankrupt, he supported his parents, made a lot of money, and spent every penny he had.

Rose inherited the "Depression mentality" from her parents, who lost everything in the Great Depression. She started working at twelve and worked her way through college and law school. She saved every penny. She was contributing toward her widowed mother's support when she met Matthew.

Matthew and Rose were instantly attracted to each other, had a whirlwind courtship and a three-month honeymoon in Europe. She was attracted to his spontaneity, his style, and his easy approach to life. He liked her seriousness, her intelligence, and her steadfast character. Besides, she was as pretty as his mother.

They bought a duplex apartment on the east side of Manhattan and within six months were in debt, in spite of the fact that they both earned good money. Rose began to see that Matthew let money slip through his fingers, as if there was no end to the supply. All the old anxieties about never having enough came up for her and she began to nag and then to chastise him. The more she complained, the more he spent.

When she threatened to leave him they started therapy. He had been in charge of paying the bills and taxes. They had no such thing as a budget, try as she did to create one.

In doing the genogram, Matthew came upon the recognition that as a little boy he had never seen his hardworking father, and to make up for their many absences, his parents had given him any material thing he wanted. He told himself that this was the way they showed their love for him. He said ruefully, "The spoiled child gets everything except what he really needs." His lavish spending was an old habit to comfort himself. Except it didn't work.

Using hypnosis, Matthew recognized the part of himself that looked to material things to substitute for the emotional poverty he had experienced, and he learned to give to himself what he really needed—new skills to build his financial and emotional life with Rose. Once Rose recognized that he could learn how to set limits for himself, she began to relax and gave up her irrational fear of "becoming a bag lady."

Rose and Matthew genuinely loved and respected each other; they were both intelligent and they weathered some tough times straightening out the money issues that had permeated every part of their life together.

In many families one person handles the finances—pays the bills, does the taxes, makes the major financial decisions. The element of control here can be a source of resentment and frustration for both spouses. Susie says, "I have to do it because my husband, Bill, never gets around to it and then we have to pay penalties. I get tired of asking him so I do it myself!" John says, "I know I have to do it because I don't trust Susie with the figures. But when I do, she complains I don't spend enough time with her and the kids, so I give up and let her do it." Susie and John and many others feel that they have to control the finances because they don't have any choice. The constant arguments and unsatisfactory arrangements can foster resentment and frustration on both sides. One partner is seen as controlling; the other as too dependent. It may get the job done, but it may not be satisfying or fulfilling.

Hypnosis can help get to the root cause of the suffering about money and reframe it, helping the person recognize when he or she is shifting into the mind-set of the frightened or suffering child and finding new ways to soothe and help it. If and when the spouse can witness this process, he or she can play an important role in the healing. Sometimes work has to be done with the spouse who may, for unconscious reasons, be contributing to the problem. That is why it is so important for both people to work together.

Money as a Trigger

For many people money issues are triggers that can activate painful childhood imprints, but they can also be the impetus for healing. A death in the family is always disruptive and throws everyone into the family trance, each member playing early childhood roles. Where finances and estates are concerned, meetings can become primitive and vicious, sometimes leading to emotional wounds that are difficult to heal.

Dorothy came to me for hypnotherapy five weeks after her father died. She was in deep mourning, which was exacerbated by her stepbrother, John, who had gone to court to have Dorothy's mother, who was ill, declared incompetent. This was not true. John's own mother had died when he was a year old and Dorothy's mother, her father's second wife, had raised him. She was a passive woman who allowed her husband and stepson to bully her.

For as long as Dorothy could remember, John had been the family troublemaker. Four years older than Dorothy, he abused her and her two younger sisters constantly. Using their mother as a model, they were all afraid of him, and because her mother was so docile Dorothy felt helpless to protect her. Dorothy's father was alternately explosive and loving. Dorothy took on her mother's passivity and was unable to defend herself against John. Even as an adult she would freeze when he started yelling at her.

Dorothy's father's death was her ultimate challenge. Now the mother of four children, she felt she had to stop her brother from taking the family estate away from her mother and, ultimately, her children. It was as if her father's death had focused all the family pain and competition onto money.

The issue of her father's estate motivated Dorothy to change her behavior. She literally could not afford to be the helpless little girl any longer. In hypnosis, she mobilized the strengths she had developed outside the family. She had been elected president of her class in high school *and* college, was a first-class athlete, and had received many awards, including Phi Beta Kappa. Her husband, Jake, an electrical engineer, was emotionally supportive, and she realized that in many ways she had the strength to cope with her brother.

She hired a lawyer, countersued her brother, and eventually won the case. Much of her work in hypnosis was with the board-of-directors exercise in chapter seven.

I told her a metaphor that meant a lot to her. It was a true story that involves role-playing. A young, passive, and frightened woman named Susannah had been a member of a group led by Virginia Satir, a pioneer family therapist. Susannah was an only child whose mother had died when she was ten. She became panic-stricken when her devoted father died and named her chairman of the board and CEO of his multimillion-dollar family corporation, with ownership of all the controlling stock. Susannah was going to have to face a phalanx of enraged family members at the board meeting the following week.

Susannah had just graduated from law school, and although she had passed the bar, she felt totally incompetent to run the family corporation. She also knew that her father's brothers were intent on wresting the company away from her. Wives, cousins, and distant relatives were all mobilizing themselves against their common enemy—Susannah.

Virginia asked Susannah to pick out members of the group to role-play her relatives and to sit them around the board of directors' table. She then asked Susannah to go out of the room and come in as if she were coming into the meeting and to do whatever she felt like doing. Susannah walked in, froze, and crawled under the table, crouching on all fours. She had to listen while the "family members" discussed exactly how they were going to get the corporation away from her.

Eventually Susannah was able to come out from under the table. Virginia helped her climb up on top of the table. From that position she role-played a confrontation with everyone around the table, looking down at them as she spoke. She called upon her love for her father for strength, and she used what she had learned practicing moot court in law school. As the day wore on, she became more sure of herself.

Susannah has been chairman of the board and CEO for twenty years and has expanded the corporation.

Dorothy used that example in her work with herself and in some role-plays she and I did with the parts of herself that were continually growing and strengthening. She is no longer afraid of John, who went into psychotherapy and has mellowed considerably as he has begun to take responsibility for his own pain.

With regard to money, both Susannah and Dorothy have been able to shift out of the family trance into the parts of themselves that had learned to function in the outside world. They also developed more compassion for the frightened little girls they had been.

Your Money and Your Life

Attitudes toward money and giving and receiving generalize to every part of our lives. A person who holds on tightly to his or her money may also hold on tightly to his or her ability to love freely. The emotional contraction generalizes to people's bodies. Often their backs and chests are tight, as are their buttocks. Emotions and physiology are expressing the same phenomenon—how we feel about ourselves. People learn from childhood experience to measure their self-esteem by the amount of money they have, don't have, inherit, or lose.

Because attitudes toward money affect every aspect of our lives and therefore of our relationships, it is vital to discover how it affects us on many levels. We may understand it in our heads, but this area is much more primitive. Hypnotic exploration can help us locate the underlying fears that characterize people's difficulties with money and that are at the roots of what causes our choices about money. Money issues can destroy a relationship; understanding and changing them can transform a relationship.

Even if you're working on yourself by yourself, it is important to look at your attitudes about money and where they come from. They can be an expression of your whole personality. Sometimes fear of loss of money is at the root of the difficulties that people have with intimacy, because they measure themselves by how much they have rather than by who they are.

▶ EXERCISE 25 ◀
FEELINGS ABOUT MONEY

Sit down in your special place with your journal, your pen, your timer, and your colored index cards in front of you. Set your timer for fifteen minutes. Close your eyes and check your inner barometer for your comfort level with yourself and with your partner. Bring yourself present and then get your journal out and write as fast as you can—without thinking too much—four phrases or sentences that describe how you feel about money.

When you have finished, mark next to each phrase or sentence a plus or a minus, representing your positive feeling about that phrase or your negative feeling about it. Notice how many are positive and how many are negative.

When you have finished, go to the beginning phrase and if it is positive, think of a situation when this phrase could be negative. If it is negative, think of a situation when it could be positive. Jot it down. Do the same with all four ideas.

For example: "I think having too much money corrupts people." That would be considered negative. To make it positive: "If you have a lot of money you can do a lot of good with it. You can give to charities, start a foundation, give to medical programs for children in Third World countries." A positive statement: "I think we should enjoy spending money wisely." This could become: "I think money is evil and we should save it all."

You don't have to be right. This is your exercise so have fun with it.

When you both have finished, put down your pen, close your eyes, set the timer for four minutes, and let your thumb and forefinger come together. Take a deep breath, hold it for the count of five, and when you exhale just enjoy relaxing and not necessarily having to think of anything. Just enjoy letting your unconscious do whatever work it wants.

At the sound of the timer, share with your partner what you have learned if you'd like.

Close your eyes and check your inner barometer for your level of comfort with yourself and with your partner.

After you have finished sharing, write down any impressions you want, and schedule your next meeting.

▶ Tool Kit

In the following week, notice any thoughts you are having about money or finance and how the two of you have been working or not working with this area of your life. Each time you handle a bill or change, let it be a reminder of what money really means to you and just notice. You might want to write down any new awarenesses you have.

▶ EXERCISE 26 ◀
MONEY AND YOUR GENOGRAM

Let yourself get comfortable in your special place. Place a copy of your family genogram in front of you, along with your journal, pen, and timer. Close your eyes for a moment and get in touch with your level of comfort with yourself and with your partner. Look at your family genogram for a while. Ask yourself about your family's rules, messages, myths, secrets, longings, and fears about money.

Then set the timer for twenty minutes, close your eyes again, let your thumb and forefinger come together, and take a deep breath. Hold it for the count of five, and then slowly exhale. Take five more comfortable breaths. Just enjoy being with yourself for a few moments.

Then open your eyes, pick up your pen and, looking at the genogram, write down each individual whose attitudes have influenced you consciously and unconsciously about money and finance. Write whatever comes to mind without censoring it. Write about their messages to you and how you have been influenced in conscious and perhaps unconscious ways. You might want to have several pages for each of these important, influential people in your background. Write down whatever you wish, because this is for you; nobody else has to see it. Then, when you are ready, share whatever you want to with your partner.

Close your eyes and check your inner barometer for your comfort level with yourself and with your partner.

▶ Tool Kit

In the following week, notice any thoughts or associations that come up with regard to money and its influence on you by your family of origin. Write down the associations you may want to remember.

▶ EXERCISE 27 ◀
THE MONEY QUESTIONNAIRE

Please let yourself get comfortable in your special place, putting your journal, pen, and timer in front of you. Set the timer for twenty minutes, or longer if you both agree.

Let your thumb and forefinger come together, take a deep breath, and hold it for the count of five. Release the breath and as you feel yourself letting go, just be with yourself, not thinking of anything in particular. Then when you are ready, pick up your pen and look at the following questions. Write down whatever comes to mind.

▶ How do you think about money? Do you enjoy thinking about it? Do you hate thinking about it?

▶ Do you feel victimized or enslaved by your thoughts about money?

▶ Can you have fun thinking about money?

▶ Name eight feelings you have about money.

▶ What are the important messages you got about money?

▶ What were your first thoughts about money?

▶ Whose attitudes influenced you most about money?

▶ Whose attitudes about money did you respect the most? Why?

▶ Do you still respect those attitudes?

▶ Whose attitudes did you respect the least about money? Why?

▶ Do you still?

▶ Has money played a part in your relationships? How so?

▶ Can you freely give and freely receive money?

▶ Do you fret or fuss about money?

▶ Do other people's attitudes about money irritate you? Do your own attitudes irritate you?

▶ Did you inherit the "Depression mentality" about money? People who lived through the Depression were often imprinted by their traumatic losses. This irrational-fear orientation can color how you make money, save it, spend it, and how you can or cannot compromise with your partner's attitudes.

▶ Are you so driven by the need to make money, save money, or spend money that you have lost real contact with yourself, your family, your friends, your joy?

▶ Is money your friend, your enemy, or a monkey on your back?

▶ Do you buy on impulse (which can be a form of anxiety)?

▶ Do you feel in control of your attitudes about money? If not, how could you get control?

▶ Is there any person or persons whose orientation to money you would like to have? Who are they? What are their attitudes?

▶ What are the obstacles to your having a creative, powerful, effective, and fulfilling relationship with money?

▶ How can you overcome them?

▶ How will you know when you have overcome them? Get in touch with what that would feel like.

When you have finished answering these questions, check your inner barometer for your level of comfort with yourself and with your partner. If you want, share your answers with your partner.

▶ Tool Kit

During the week, notice any other attitudes that you have about money that you may not have identified yet and write them down. Notice any change in your behavior about money.

▶ EXERCISE 28 ◀
USING WHAT YOU HAVE LEARNED
TO RESOLVE DISPUTES ABOUT MONEY

At first glance you may have complex feelings about doing this exercise and I encourage you to be curious about how your arguments will be affected. There is much to gain when you try to do something different.

Go to your special place with your journal, pen, the sheets of paper on which you each wrote the levels of the iceberg, and your timer. Set the timer for thirty minutes. Get comfortable and be with yourself for a few moments. Then ask yourself: "What are the most difficult areas of disagreement with my partner about money?" If you are doing this alone, ask yourself: "What are the parts of myself that are in conflict about money?" Write down whatever comes to mind. Then get in touch with your inner barometer and check your comfort level with yourself and with your partner.

When you are ready, let your thumb and forefinger come together, close your eyes, and take a deep breath. Hold it for the count of five and then let it go and let go of all the tension that can just flow out of your body easily and comfortably. When you are ready, open your eyes and add anything more to the list that you might want to.

Stand facing each other and lay out the sheets of paper that list the levels of the iceberg. Each of you stands on your sheet of paper marked "Behavior." The partner with the darkest hair, *A,* goes first and shares the most difficult and disturbing problem or problems that he or she feels about how the two of you handle money.

Each partner steps sideways onto the sheet marked "Stances," facing each other, and *A* says, "I think that when I become a_____ and_____, you become a_____and_____."

B then steps on the "Stances" sheet and says, "When you think you become a_____and_____, I become a_____and _____."

Each partner then steps sideways onto the sheet marked "Feelings," facing each other, and *A* says: "What I feel about this behavior is_____."

B listens without interrupting and then says: "I appreciate that is how you feel. What I feel is_____."

Each partner then steps sideways onto the sheet marked "Feelings About Feelings." *A* says: "What I feel about my feelings is_____." *B* says: "I appreciate that is how you feel about your feelings. What I feel about my feelings is_____."

Then each of you bends down and picks up the sheet marked "Stances." Turn back to back. *A* says: "How I am trying to cope with this is by _[behavior]_." *B* says: "How I am trying to cope with this is by _[behavior]_."

Then each partner picks up the sheet marked "Perceptions" and goes to the opposite corner of the room. *A* says: "What I believe about what is happening is_____." *B* says: "What I believe about what is happening is_____."

Each partner then turns to face the wall. *A* says, "My underneath

165

assumption is _____." *B* says: "My underneath assumption is _____."

Both of you come to the middle of the room facing each other and pick up the sheet marked "Expectations." *A* says: "My unfulfilled expectation is _____." *B* says: "My unfulfilled expectation is _____."

Now kneel, facing each other, and pick up the paper that says "Need for Love." *A* says: "My need for love is expressed by my _____." *B* says: "My need for love is expressed by my _____."

Then sit facing each other, pick up the paper marked "Core Self," and hold hands if you want to. *A* says: "I am not my yearning. I have the yearning and all the rest of it, and I am more than that." *B* says: "I am not my yearning. I have the yearning and all the rest of it, and I am more than that."

When you have finished, close your eyes and be with yourself. Then open your eyes and write in your journal whatever comes up for you. Check your inner barometer for your comfort level with yourself and with your partner.

When you are finished, share with your partner whatever you would like.

If you are doing this alone, go through the exercise and say each statement aloud to yourself. After each statement, let your eyes close, let your thumb and forefinger come together, take a deep breath, count to five, exhale, and repeat the statement silently to yourself. Follow the instructions for your change of body positions and continue with the statements in the same manner.

When you have finished, close your eyes and be with yourself. Then open your eyes and write in your journal whatever comes up for you. Check your inner barometer for your comfort level with each part of yourself.

▶ Variation on the Theme

After you have done the first part of this exercise, you may want to repeat it with the following change:

This time have an argument about the same topic without using the sheets of paper on which the iceberg levels are written. Follow the sequence of moving. Continue this sequence of changing positions while you argue until you have a breakthrough, or you get tired or bored or you come up with some kind of interim resolution. *Continue this sequence of movement until something constructive happens.*

Then when you sit down together, map out how each of you will change your behavior in some important way. Plan to meet every two weeks for an hour or so to go over money, budget, and finance matters, and to evaluate the changes you have made. This meeting should be in some place other than your special place to work on your relationship. It should not be in a car and it should not be in the bedroom. Pick a neutral place.

If you are working alone, here is a model for working alone with parts of yourself:

Place two chairs facing each other with a table in between. Each chair represents a part of you that is in conflict. When you start your budget review, sit in one chair and say what you feel and what you want and write it down. Then change to the other chair that represents a part that disagrees and say what that part feels and wants and write it down. Continue this back-and-forth exercise, negotiating and making refinements in what you write down. Notice what you are feeling as you do this exercise and at the end of the exercise write down what you have discovered. Commit yourself to doing this someplace other than your special place for one hour every two weeks.

When you have finished this exercise, check your inner barometer for your comfort level with yourself and with your partner. Notice if there is a change.

▶ Tool Kit

Notice during the week whatever comes up around money and finances and jot it down. Stay committed to your outside money meeting with your partner, or, if you are doing this alone, have your meeting with the parts of yourself that were in conflict.

10

Sex: The Ultimate Trance and How to Create Long-Term Passion and Playfulness

When we were infants, every time we woke up we opened our eyes to the world around us with freshness and wonder. We drank in all that we saw and heard and touched. Our unconscious absorbed everything. Our sense of smell was acute. Think of a favorite aroma that you loved as a kid and notice how that fragrance brings back a full memory of a place, a person, a feeling. Think of someone you love. Does that person have a special smell to you—perfume? shaving cream? sweat?

The infant is intensely attuned to the mother—the sound of her voice, the expression in her eyes, the smell of her, the touch of her. This exquisite sensitivity is part of the first experience of bonding, of love, and is the foundation of our ability to love. This ability to love is associated with whatever imprinting occurred in the mind of the infant or growing child.

When couples fall in love, they tune in to each other on the same exquisitely sensitive frequencies that they experienced in themselves as children. The intensity of feeling amplifies their pleasure. But it also increases their vulnerability.

It is this vulnerability to imprinting that brings to the surface the unresolved original family conflicts and fears, which may long ago have been consciously forgotten.

Sally Lou was so wild about her husband, Joseph, that it wasn't until several months after they were married that she began to realize that he never arrived home when he said he would. He was always late. She had never noticed this before, but now it bothered her. He was exactly like her father, and all she could ever hear were her mother's endless complaints—"Your father never does what he says he is going to do!" Her mother's frustration was so painful to little Sally Lou that she had blocked it. Now she was seeing her father's behavior in her new husband and the long years of her mother's disappointment stretched out in front of her.

The magic of couples' discovery of each other can begin to tarnish not only in their daily activities together but also in their nightly connections. The bedroom is often the first place that unrecognized difficulties can show up because of the intimacy of their sexual connection.

While how we talk to each other has profound effects on our bodies and our feelings, how we touch each other is even more compelling. One touch from a person can tell you more than a thousand words. Our skin picks up subtle messages. A limp handshake can tell you much about a person; a steely grip tells you something else. A handshake that is firm and gentle is different from a handshake that barely touches you and is withdrawn, and that is different from the handshake that holds on to your hand long into the conversation. That handshake may tell you a lot about the person, or it may tell you what the person is trying to convey to you.

The art of touching in lovemaking can make all the difference.

How we receive the touching also makes all the difference. When we are connected to our whole selves our touch conveys the full message. When we are distracted, compartmentalized, or not "in the moment," touch becomes meaningless and automatic. Lovemaking is usually not loving when you are angry. You may experience orgasm, but you may have turned off your deeper emotions.

Your touch conveys many levels of your inner experience. Our skin is an organ that picks up subliminal messages and is reactive to the subtleties of touch. Touch your own hand as lightly as you can and stroke it. Close your eyes and notice what you are feeling. Then grab one hand with the other tightly and notice what you feel. Multiply those differences a hundred times and you may get a sense of the variety of messages your skin takes in every time you are touched or touch someone else. Often these messages are unconscious and you may not be aware of them at all—until you learn to "listen" to your own listening skin. Anger, anxiety, and frustration all are powerfully conveyed by touch, outside of our conscious awareness. And these emotions can affect our perception of touch.

Ilana Rubenfeld, who has developed a system called the Rubenfeld Synergy Method that uses touch for healing purposes, has pointed out that when you touch someone you help them go into trance. That connection goes directly to the unconscious. Ilana has said, "I know that if I am not comfortable with all parts of myself, I cannot really connect with another person." Feldenkrais, an Israeli physicist who did hypnosis with the body, said that touch connects the unconscious of one person with the unconscious of another. This means that when we touch each other we can put each other into trance and connect on very deep levels. However, if you are not fully connected to yourself, you will be unable to connect with someone else or even be aware of what your touch is conveying to another person.

Deede, a social worker, told me, "I know I married Rob on the rebound from a passionate, turbulent relationship. Rob was so kind and thoughtful and a really good friend. We liked the same things and we went well together. Our relationship was peaceful, but there was no passion.

"Now, after three years of marriage, I still don't really know what Rob feels. He never gets angry at me, but he put his fist through a wooden panel last month. And when he touches me I feel nothing from him. Sex is mechanistic, predictable, and no fun. I know what is going to happen, and even if I have an orgasm, I just want to get it over with. I miss the deep passion I had for Tony, though we couldn't live together!"

Rob, an army colonel, had been raised in the military and graduated from West Point at the head of his class. His mother was the perfect wife. She took the "obey" instruction in her marriage vows very seriously and demanded the same behavior from her four children.

When Rob looked at his family history he recognized how "impeccable" it was. There was minimal feeling expressed and no joy or fun at all. The language he knew was "to respect and obey." As an army brat, Rob had lived all over the world. As soon as he made new friends, the family was moved to the next military assignment. Correct behavior and discipline made family life humorless and strict. He never wanted to go to West Point but was too afraid of his father to go out on his own.

Doubts and disagreements under the surface manifest in the intimate dance of sexual intercourse. Deede wanted a baby, but Rob was ambivalent. He discovered that he really did not want to have a family like the one he grew up in. He was terrified because he felt he was beginning to live the same life as his father. For sure, this was not what he wanted! Rob had lost all desire for his wife because his unconscious reluctance to start a family had caused him to draw back from her sexually. His fears inhibited his sexual behavior and Deede felt this as a lack of passion in their marriage.

Deede was not aware of Rob's fear. All she knew was that their sex life was unfulfilling. She said, "I don't feel like we are making love. We are just fucking—and it is not even great fucking at that."

In therapy together, Rob admitted that his secret dream was to leave the military and go into business for himself in something related to skiing. Deede also loved the outdoors and was an avid skier. She also admitted she didn't like the demands of military life. As they began to share their real feelings with each other—neither of them really enjoyed the careers they had chosen—they began to choreograph a life together that fulfilled them both. It took some planning and a lot of work. As time went on and they each uncovered the feelings that they both had suppressed to "protect" the other, their sex life improved. As the rigidity of their life together loosened up, their sexual activity came alive.

Our Unconscious Fears Can Create Havoc in the Bedroom

Remember Sandra and Charlie in chapter six? Their sex life had stopped and Sandra had moved out of the bedroom. In therapy, Charlie, who had grown up in a family of boys who enjoyed fighting, worked hard to get in touch with his gentleness, which he had buried to protect himself in his family of origin. I told him a story I had heard about Marlon Brando that fascinated him. Before his role as Stanley in *A Streetcar Named Desire*, Brando was slender and quite sensitive-looking. He built up his body for the role, and to prepare for Stanley's animal toughness, he spent many days with the stevedores down on the New York docks. He noticed that their hands were so callused that at dinner, if they knocked over a saltshaker or an empty beer mug, they didn't even notice. Brando wanted to portray that kind of insensitivity.

Charlie, whose hands were big and callused, was interested in that story and the fact that the stevedores were unaware of what they touched. He turned to Sandra and asked her, "Do I touch you too hard?" She fumbled for words and I encouraged her to tell him the truth. She nodded and Charlie, instead of getting angry and defensive, asked shyly, "Would you show me how you want me to touch you?" It took some time, but eventually they moved back into the same bed.

Charlie and Sandra developed an understanding of how their original family relationships had affected their sexual behavior, and how, because they were both so vulnerable, they had each blamed the other unfairly. Sandra had tried to be a "saint" like her mother, and never showed her feelings, even when her alcoholic father hit her. Charlie, who came from a family whose major mode of communication was anger, blamed Sandra for her depression, and as she got in touch with the anger and expressed it, he became more angry and anxious, which frightened her. As they came to understand the original causes of much of their miscommunication, they each became more sensitive to the vulnerability in the other. Sandra understood that Charlie's roughness was a mask for his sensitivity; Charlie recognized that being gentle and tender did not mean he was weak. That kind of understanding can certainly free up lovemaking!

Andrea and Steven met in college, went to law school, went to work for two prestigious law firms, and had been living together for nine years. They both had the same goals of becoming partner and having an affluent lifestyle. Neither wanted children because "we don't want to do to a child what was done to us." Their life together worked well—until they decided to get married.

The ceremony was elegant, tasteful, and small; the honeymoon on St. John's was luxurious. They settled into married life, and then gradually, in little incremental details, life began to become humdrum and boring for each of them.

"I know him so well I don't even look forward to seeing him anymore. He is doing better at work and I am afraid I might not make partner!" Andrea said. "I will not be like my mother and stay in the shadow of a powerful man and then watch while he leaves me for a twenty-year-old trophy wife!"

Steven said, "I can't understand Andrea. We were always so happy until we got married. She is becoming more and more distant!"

Sometimes when couples who have lived together for a long time get married, the specter of marriage descends upon them like a ghost from the past. Which, of course, it is. Often their image of marriage is not conscious so they can't understand what happened. And often the first place problems show up is in the bedroom. It is hard for people to see how their associations with the idea of marriage, which they learned as children, can affect the relationship that has worked very well until their marriage vows.

Andrea's mother was a beautiful woman who worked hard at maintaining her youth and good looks. Andrea said that her mother had made a career out of being beautiful, and she suspected that her mother did not enjoy her body sexually because she was so "fastidious" and "never would talk to me about sex. I had to learn from my nanny and at school." Andrea made up her mind when she was eight years old that she would have a career and contribute something to the world. She couldn't compete with her mother's polished beauty, so she wouldn't even try. She had become sexually active at seventeen, one year before she met Steven. She had always enjoyed sex and could not understand what happened to her after she and Steven got married.

In hypnosis, she remembered many statements her mother had made about the necessity of keeping a man interested because men couldn't be trusted. As her mother got older, she held on to her beauty rituals more desperately, and Andrea watched helplessly as her mother became more and more depressed and began to drink heavily, and eventually divorced her husband after he left her for another woman. Some part of Andrea's mind had associated this denouement with the act of marriage, and although she had always trusted Steven, her body no longer could respond to him with the familiar freedom she had always known.

Steven, who thought he had married this strong, independent woman, was at a loss. When they came into treatment they had not had sex for six months, although they had previously been very active.

Andrea had heard all her life about how men cannot be trusted, that marriage is precarious. Her unconscious fear that Steven might leave her, as her father had left her mother, seeped into the bedroom and it was difficult for her to let him touch her. When she realized these feelings and shared them with Steven and he accepted them, her coldness melted and she was able to enjoy sex again.

Sexual Vulnerability

Sexual intercourse is the joining of two people on many levels—especially the deep, vulnerable core self that is at the bottom of our iceberg of consciousness. We let go into a rhythmic pulsation that some poets say flows at the source of the life energy of the universe. Think of your most intense and vulnerable orgasmic connection with someone and notice the tender, vulnerable feelings the thought can evoke—even tears. It can be a great awakening into a new internal spaciousness—especially if it continues over time in the lives of a couple who live together.

This is what trance is all about. Each person accessing the deepest part of himself or herself and sharing it without reservation—fully in the moment.

William Masters, M.D., author of *Human Sexual Response,* said, "Love is the exchange of vulnerability." This is not easy for people who have spent their lives protecting their vulnerability.

Performance anxiety occurs when the critical self-observer intrudes. Dr. Masters told of twin brothers who celebrated their fortieth birthday together with their wives and had too much champagne to drink. Neither could perform sexually that night. At breakfast the next morning the first brother apologized profusely to his wife and began to worry about his subsequent performance. The second brother also apologized and said that he had had too much to drink, "but I will make it up to you." He didn't worry about it and subsequently performed just fine. The first brother began to obsess to the point that he developed problems with having an erection and went to the doctor. This was probably because he was so busy watching himself he couldn't really be with his body's experience.

The most sensitive and vulnerable part of each of us is our sexual part. Women who have been sexually abused are particularly fearful and often emotionally and physically scarred. One of Erickson's most famous cases was a suicidal psychologist who had been brought to him by a concerned friend. "I saw her only once," he told us. The woman, we'll call her Nancy, was twenty-eight. She had been sexually penetrated by her father from age five to sixteen, when she left home. She was severely depressed and had no feeling in her genitals. She decided to go to college and graduate school so that she would feel better about herself. She avoided men altogether because she was terrified of a "big, bold, erect penis." When she got her graduate degree and set up her practice, she felt no better about herself, so she became a prostitute and let pimps do whatever they wanted with her.

When she was brought to Erickson she was acutely suicidal. Erickson worked with her, helping her go into trance, and then said to her, "I think you are very silly! [That got her attention.] Don't you know that you have a vagina that can take a vicious pleasure in reducing the biggest, boldest, most erect penis to a helpless dangling object very promptly." There was a twinkle in his eye as he told us the story. "I said vicious pleasure!"

She went away and several months later he got a letter from her saying that she had taken his advice and had experienced vicious pleasure in reducing several big, bold, erect penises to helpless dangling objects very promptly. The vicious pleasure became pleasure and now she was staying celibate until she found "the right man" with whom she could enjoy a mutually gratifying relationship.

This story is an example of a reframe, and I have told it to many women who froze at the thought of sexual intercourse. There are many appropriate times when this story can help. Women who have been sexually abused or raped feel helpless and victimized on a primitive, molecular level. The body's memory of the experience is a powerful imprint that can take over and paralyze the woman emotionally and physically. To a woman who has been victimized, the new thought that her vagina is powerful can give her a new sense of herself.

When I think it would be appropriately received and not seen as implied criticism or as incongruent with their feelings about men, I sometimes tell women about a client of mine who loves being a woman. She believes that her body is a vessel and that her husband, whom she loves deeply, can come there and be refreshed and revitalized. She feels that she is like an oasis in the desert of his working life. In addition, she enjoys her own lusty appetite. She says she is like a pussycat in the kitchen and a tiger in the bedroom.

Some male clients have experienced ejaculation as a weakening of their male strength—as if the woman's body were sucking his very essence from him. It is important for such a man to look carefully at where he got that feeling. Often it is a little boy's fearful fantasies about a dominating or narcissistic mother who uses him emotionally to satisfy her ego. It is hard for a man to get past that specter in the back of his mind so that he can enjoy being a masterful and tender lover. But it is not impossible. Using hypnosis, he can separate his little-boy experiences with his mother from his adult relationships with women. Seeing his mother from a different perspective can help him free the feelings that have restricted his ability to express his whole self.

We are all sensitive about our own sexuality. Sometimes when we talk to each other we amplify our sensitivity: "I love you to stroke me lightly right here, under my arm" can be felt as an implied criticism and can quench the flow of feeling before it even gets started. "Did you *really* come?" is a question that can give her the feeling he doesn't trust her—or worse, if she *was* faking it, could make her feel ashamed, unmasked, and even more vulnerable.

It is not so much what we say as how we say it. Sometimes it is better to show your partner. For example: "I love it when you do this." And she takes his hand and strokes under her arm gently. "Are you fully satisfied or do you want more?" probably works better than asking if she had orgasm.

Getting in Touch with Your Lover and Yourself

In the movie *Don Juan DeMarco*, Marlon Brando, an aging psychiatrist about to retire, reconnects with his early ardor for his wife of thirty-five years. At the very end of the film, he says to his wife as they sit in the garden, "I need to find out who you are!" She replies, "Who has brought you coffee for the last thirty-five years?" He says, "I know a lot about dirty coffee cups and facts. . . . I want to know what your hopes and dreams were when I got lost along the way when I was thinking about myself!" She begins to cry and says, "I thought you would never ask!" It is a beautiful moment, but what about those previous thirty-five years?

When you look back at your relationship, do you have moments like these? You can create them so they can evoke your deeper connections with each other. Staying committed to your own hopes, wishes, and dreams, and sharing them, makes it possible to stay closer to your partner's hopes, wishes, and dreams.

In the Masters and Johnson course in human sexuality, couples learn to develop what is called "sensate focus." In the first sessions of a two-week program they are sent back to their hotel rooms and instructed to learn more about their partner's body just by touch. They are instructed not to have orgasm. They are told to just discover their bodies by lightly touching and savoring their partner's body in places they had not explored before.

This intense focus on making delicate distinctions through touch and receiving the sensation without judgment is what trance is all about. Remember, trance is highly focused attention, moving with the flow of feeling, sensation, imagery, or just drifting in and out of your experience, feeling comfortable and connected to the movement and the changes. With practice you can learn to move into the rhythmic dance together.

Full sexual expression correlates with full self-expression. A person who represses or suppresses anger will also repress or suppress sexual expression. When the suppression-repression button goes on in any area of a relationship, it goes on in the sexual relationship. That is why it is imperative that a couple explores their attitudes about sex and their sexual relationship. When the deeper problems that may be underground surface early and are dealt with, the couple can create many future hours of pleasure instead of pain.

Using what you have practiced in all the previous exercises— getting in touch with your inner barometer and noticing the degree of comfort with yourself and with your partner—you can discover if there is a glitch. Pay attention to it as it happens, accept it, and talk about it if you can. Awareness of your body and your feelings is what is most important.

▶ EXERCISE 29 ◀
THE INTIMACY QUESTIONNAIRE

Settle into the special space you share together and put your journal and a pen or pencil next to you. Close your eyes, let your thumb and forefinger come together, and take a deep breath. Hold it for the count of five and as you let it go, go to that safe place of yours inside your mind, or make up a new safe place. Allow yourself to enjoy becoming more comfortable with the sensations of that place as you breathe them in.

Check your inner barometer for your comfort level with yourself and with your partner.

Take a few moments, and then when you are ready, open your eyes, pick up your pen, and write down your thoughts in response to the following questions. Answer the questions as fast as you can, letting go of thinking too much. Let your inner critic relax and take a vacation. There are no right answers—only your answers. These questions are designed to help you discover any hidden thoughts, associations, and feelings you may have. Becoming more clear about them may help you to know the sexual part of yourself better.

- What is your first memory of your mother's feelings about her sexuality?
- What is your first memory of your father's feelings about his sexuality?
- What is your first memory of your sibling's (or siblings') feelings about his/her sexuality?
- What is your first memory of your own feelings about your sexuality?
- What are your associations with how the people around you felt about their sexuality?
- Were your feelings different? The same?
- Were they comfortable? Uncomfortable?
- How did growing up in your particular family affect your experience of your own sexuality?
- How did the experiences outside your family affect your experience of your own sexuality?
- What or who helped you feel good about your sexual self, even honor it? What or who helped you to distrust your sexual self?

▶ What feelings did you have about your genitals? Did you like them? Do you like them now?

▶ Were you glad about being the sex you are? Are you glad now?

▶ Were you confused about your sexuality? Did you feel confident? Embarrassed? Ashamed?

▶ Are you uncomfortable answering these questions, even to yourself? How do you know you are uncomfortable and where is it in your body? (If you are uncomfortable, take a deep breath and go back into your safe place for a few minutes.)

▶ What are your memories of your family's conversations about sex? Were they comfortable? Uncomfortable? Were you part of the conversation? Did you feel invisible? Did you wish you were invisible during those moments?

▶ How did your family's language about sex influence you?

▶ How did the language of people outside your family influence you?

▶ What were your first romantic fantasies?

▶ What were your first sexual fantasies?

▶ Who was your first love? Was it reciprocated?

▶ Was your first love a happy experience? Unhappy? Bittersweet? What did you tell yourself about it?

▶ What were your feelings about your feelings?

▶ What did you tell yourself about your experience? Did your first experience affect your subsequent experience with love and your sexual expression?

▶ As you look back over your lifetime experience with love and sexuality, do you notice any patterns? How were your relationships similar or different? How did they reflect patterns in your family of origin?

▶ When you think of your current relationship, how is it similar or different from the relationships you have had in the past?

▶ How has what you learned from your past relationships affected your present relationship?

▶ As you think about it now, how has your present relationship changed or transformed your experience of your sexual self? What has been rewarding and enriching about your relationship with your partner? If you would like to enrich and deepen this part of your self-expression even more, what in yourself would you need to explore? Are you willing to? When?

▶ Can you comfortably share these thoughts with your partner? Are you in the habit of sharing with your partner the good things you have together, as well as the bad? If not, what gets in the way? Does it come from automatic behaviors you learned in the past? Take a look. Maybe you need to write your thoughts down first. Maybe you need some professional help with becoming clear about just what you need to say. If you are afraid that what you might say might hurt or push away your partner, where did you learn to withhold? Do you say to yourself that perhaps it is the better part of wisdom to maintain the status quo? Is that what you want?

Check your inner barometer for your comfort level with yourself and with your partner.

▶ Tool Kit

In the following week you might look over the questions again. Notice if any thoughts or memories that might have been stimulated by these questions come up. If so, write them down. Notice any changes in your sexual behavior.

▶ **EXERCISE 30** ◀
SELF-REFLECTIONS

There was a cartoon in *The New Yorker* many years ago that showed a medieval knight sitting on a stone bench by a pond gazing intently at his reflection in the water. Leaning on his arm, gazing lovingly into his profile, a beautiful young maiden is saying, "I think there is something that is coming between us, Narcissus!"

There might not be much of a difference between the way Narcissus looks at himself and the way some people judge themselves sexually. Self-judgment, whether positive or negative, gets in the way of real connection in a relationship. It is one thing to accept and enjoy yourself so completely that you can be totally in the moment; it is another to keep evaluating yourself or your behavior so that you cannot be completely a part of your experience. Which do you do?

In the following meditation it is important that you simply watch without judgment. Just observe the thoughts, images, associations, and memories while they move across the horizon of your mind, as if they were clouds in the sky, drifting, changing, dissolving.

Check your inner barometer for your comfort level with yourself and with your partner.

Before you start, let your hands clasp each other the way you learned in chapter two, exercise three (page 37), to remind yourself to use the nonhabitual clasp. Unclasp your hands.

Now let your thumb and forefinger come together, press very tightly, and take a deep breath. Hold it for a count of five, and when you let go, let go of all the tension in your body. Pay attention to becoming more and more comfortable with each breath you take. Then go to your safe place and just enjoy what you are seeing, hearing, feeling, touching, tasting, and smelling.

When you are fully there, ask your inner mind to reconnect you with an early feeling of love and sexual stirring that you found delightful, comforting, warm, exciting. When you are with that memory, let your hands come together in the nonhabitual way and breathe in that lovely feeling. If you cannot find that feeling, make up a picture that delights you, or hear some music that gives you a good feeling and just be with that.

Unclasp your hands. Think of another time when you felt fulfilled and happy inside and again let your hands come together in that particular way. Repeat this several times with different memories.

(If you cannot locate past moments when your body felt wonderfully satisfied, ask your unconscious to make it up. Picture some time in the future when you can feel really satisfied and happy in your body. If that doesn't help, pick a part of your body, any part, and give it permission to relax into a state of comfort and pleasure. It can even be your little finger or your belly button. With practice you may even learn to get this feeling of pleasure to radiate throughout your whole body! Give it a try. It can help.)

Now go back to the first time you met your partner. What happened between the two of you that attracted you? Was it instantaneous or did it grow? What specifically drew you to this person? The tone of voice, the sparkle in the eyes, the way the body moved? Let yourself recall the first sexual encounter you had together. Get in touch with the experiences that had meaning for you. Reexperience them in your mind and in your body. If negative moments that are more recent intrude, just observe them without judgment and watch them dissolve. Then, when it is comfortable, go back to another experience with your partner that had meaning for you. Just let it happen. Your body knows how to feel.

Take as long as you want, and each time something satisfying happens clasp your hands together in that particular way. Then, when you are ready, come back to the room, pick up your pen, and write in your journal. If you want to share with your partner, take the time to do that.

Go to your inner barometer and check your comfort level with yourself and with your partner.

▶ Tool Kit

During the next week, notice and track any new pleasant and/or sexual feelings you have. Notice if and when your sexual behavior is changing. Write in your journal whatever comes up for you.

▶ EXERCISE 31 ◀
THE INTRUDERS

Settle into your special place together and let your thumb and fore-finger come together. Take a deep breath and hold it for a count of five. As you let it go, feel comfort and relaxation fill your body. When you are ready, open your eyes and write down whatever thoughts you have about the disappointing aspects of your sex life with your partner.

As you write, notice what patterns or associations emerge that you may not have been so clear about before. Go past the language of your arguments ("You always . . ." "You never . . .") to the vulnerabilities and fears behind the words. Notice what you are feeling as you write. Check your inner barometer for your comfort level with yourself and with your partner.

Go back to the previous exercise (Self-Reflections) and repeat that lesson in full. When you have finished, write down your thoughts, and if you want to, share with your partner.

▶ Tool Kit

During the following week, notice any changes in how you are thinking and/or feeling about your sexual history and your sexual re-lationship with your partner. Notice if and when your sexual behavior is changing. Write them down, even if they make no sense to you.

Pay more attention to the distinctions you can make when you touch something: the texture, the heaviness, the temperature of a fork that you pick up in a restaurant, the roughness or smoothness of your partner's skin in some area you have never thought about before. You can train yourself to make exquisite distinctions in what you sense in your everyday life.

▶ EXERCISE 32 ◀
PATTERN INTERRUPTION:
POETRY AND PLAY

This exercise is designed to access the best part of yourself—your child part. Do you remember the games you used to play as a kid? Remember the belly laughs, the jokes, the crazy behavior, the fantasies about love and kissing and what you were going to be when you grew up? Even the grimmest childhood has secret moments when that light-filled energy is present. This child part is the most wonderful, delightful part that you can bring to your sexual behavior. As children, most of us wanted to taste everything, touch everything, feel everything. That part may have been "civilized," but it is still there.

So settle into your special place with your journal and your pen and set your timer for twenty minutes. Check your inner barometer and then let your thumb and forefinger come together. Take a deep breath, hold it for the count of five, and as you let it go, just relax into a lovely feeling of comfort. Let your mind float as your body relaxes. Go to your safe place and let yourself take delight in the feeling of letting go.

Then go back to a time when you discovered a book or a poem or something that gave you a special, delightful feeling of lightness and discovery. Perhaps it was a song, or maybe a nursery rhyme that was read to you. Maybe it was a book in the library you discovered all by yourself. Maybe it was the first time you received a flower when you were invited to a school dance or it was that first tuxedo you wore, or your first kiss. Maybe you read aloud a story you wrote and brought tears to someone's eyes. Maybe you fixed something for somebody. Maybe you made up a joke and everyone laughed. Let your mind just wander to these early memories of longing and laughter.

And there are other memories not so comfortable—the other side of the coin. The first time you were rejected, a teacher's harshness, losing a baseball game, losing a friend. Let your mind move through these perhaps long-forgotten memories. Just notice them.

Take as long as you need in the time that you have and then write down whatever comes to you—perhaps moments you have never thought of before.

Then share with your partner some of those early simple childhood moments—even moments that might embarrass or sadden you, moments you have never shared with anybody. Let that special, spontaneous, deep, vulnerable, sensitive, humorous, shy, feisty, naughty part express itself.

You may feel like touching each other, holding each other's hands, or massaging each other lightly. If it is comfortable, just look into your partner's eyes as you tell your simple story and as you listen.

When you have both finished, close your eyes and go back to your safe place for a while. When you open your eyes, you can write down any thoughts that come to you and, if you wish, share them. Check your inner barometer for your comfort level with yourself and with your partner.

▶ Tool Kit

During the next week, notice other childhood memories that may emerge and write them down. Notice that childlike quality of lightness you may feel now and then.

Looking to the Future:
Two Steps Forward,
One Step Back

A s you have moved through this book you have read about how people shift into trance states in which they hear words and store them at an unconscious level; how they are imprinted by early experience in their families of origin; how these imprints organize their thinking and feeling about themselves and their relationships; and how we all talk to ourselves on unrecognized levels. You have read about the layers of our unconscious experience and how we are all made up of many parts that can be in harmony or in conflict. You have read about the struggle that many couples have with money and sexuality. You also read about your own unconscious, which some people refer to as essence, others as your special spirit. Your core self is connected to this part.

You have done exercises throughout that are designed to help you learn the things you have read by experiencing them for yourself, in your own way and in your own time. These processes are designed to continue after you finish the book and complete the exercises.

It takes three to four weeks to install a new habit. Spending a moment checking with your inner barometer for your comfort level three or four times a day would automatically become a habit over the four-week period. Your self-awareness could then become a habit that would contribute to yourself and your relationship.

It is said that you never step into the same river twice. Not only do we change in response to the flow of the river we step into, we change in response to the flow of words and touch that move between ourselves and our partners. As with everything in life, we move and change. Our partners change. We are all in constant movement—hearts beating, thoughts dancing, ideas germinating. In this movement you may find that as a couple or as a person, you occasionally take two steps forward and one step back. This is normal; old habits die hard. That backward step can be an important part of your learning. When you move forward again you can be aware of how you did it.

These exercises have been designed to help you become more aware of the flow of the river of your life—its momentum, speed, texture, your effect on it and its effect on you. Nothing ever stays still. It moves in some direction. In physics, every action causes a reaction. We change each other from moment to moment.

Sometimes the question is how to get back onto the track so you can continue to grow and deepen your ability to live your life fully. The best reinforcement is to recognize and accept what you have learned about yourself. You did the work and I hope that you appreciate that committed part of yourself. Can you breathe easier? Do you feel better about yourself? Have you become more self-aware? If so, congratulations are in order. The strongest motivator to continuing your commitment to yourself is that you have experienced value, relief, and your ability to enjoy being you. Joy brings health and love. You are the creator of your own joy.

If you feel that you are not there yet, take heart. Commit yourself to continuing these exercises or your own version of them. I suggest that you and your partner set aside two hours twice a month for six months to review what you have done and/or to redo the exercises and notice the changes. Commitment to this schedule will amplify whatever your successes have been. During the six months following your twice-a-month meeting, meet once a month. At the end of a year notice how far you have come together.

And as you feel the changes in the flow of energy between you, at the moment when you feel the backward pull, talk it over together and go back to one or another of the exercises. You may notice when you repeat an exercise after a period of time that you discover new awarenesses and you experience yourself more deeply. Your inner mind is constantly in process, and each time you tap into it, it becomes richer, more insightful, and more fulfilling.

If you choose, you can go back to these exercises periodically; each time you do will offer new experience and new growth. Just as we have stages of development as we grow from infancy to old age, so a marriage has stages of growth in which each partner undergoes changes in thinking and feeling. Using what you have learned, there are ways to weather these times of change. As you move through the inevitable transitions during your marriage, the first thing to remember is that it is important to use your ability to be as honest as you can with each other. The second is to know when you are going through a transition, because these times require special care and special awareness.

While the journey of every couple is unique, there are general stages of transition: The first is getting married and the new and fresh experience of getting to know this person who is now your spouse. Getting to know more about this person you have married may have some surprises, even if you have lived together. He may start leaving his dirty socks on the floor, or she may run to her mother's more frequently.

The second stage is the settling-in period. The arrival of children brings new responsibilities and burdens that may reawaken old unresolved family-of-origin issues that may get played out in the new family. A new personality has joined your relationship and created a new dynamic. Sometimes it is difficult for one or both partners to become used to the needs, demands, and interruptions that occur. The baby brings joy, fulfillment, and a lot of dirty diapers.

The third stage is moving into middle age and all the symbolic meanings it brings to people. If you have children, you have to cope with adolescents, which may bring up painful memories of your own adolescence. You begin facing the empty nest. At the end of this stage people often feel like they are meeting their partner again for the first time.

The fourth stage is moving into retirement and "slowing down." This could be a romantic and fun period when children have grown and grandchildren are a delight, but not as much of an energy drain as their parents might have been. It can mean a fresh start for a couple that has weathered the bad times with the good.

The fifth stage is more "slowing down." Sometimes there is illness or the loss of a spouse. This stage is marked by memories of special moments, reawakened appreciation of time, becoming gentler, perhaps being closer to nature and the beauty of small things that people never had time to absorb.

12

From Falling in Love to Growing in Love

Since every relationship is unique, you may have your own variation of transition points along the way. Two things happen in life for sure—change and suffering. The task is to bring as much joy into life as we can. Wit, humor, and laughter are great gifts. Sometimes a well-timed joke or a witty observation can interrupt what could become a dark and dreary moment. Sometimes nothing need be said, but a look or a touch can bypass a catastrophe. The tone of voice and/or the presence of another human being can mean everything in our difficult moments.

I have found that couples who learn how to give random gifts to each other, especially in the tough times, have the best chance of staying afloat on the stormy seas. I am a great believer in random gifts given for no reason at all. They don't have to be lavish or complicated. A flower, a poem, a surprise dinner of a favorite food, a trip on a ferry, a night away from home in a special hotel with room service, a stay at a bed-and-breakfast, a good joke told at the right moment—or anything else you can dream up.

I had a client, Sara, whose husband had died. What she remembered deeply and with joy was that every birthday she would wake up to find "schmaltzy" cards all over—under her pillow, by her toothbrush, in the shower, at her place at breakfast. A large gardenia plant was always delivered, and when he could, her husband would take the day off from work to be with her for a whole schedule of surprise activities. Another client received one flower every week from her husband for thirty-five years. Small moments can make a big difference.

Sometimes spontaneity can help people weather transitions. Going for a walk in a summer rainstorm, taking off on Friday afternoon for a surprise weekend, learning English country dancing together.

▶ **EXERCISE 33** ◀
REVIEWING YOUR PROGRESS

I hope the self-reflection you practiced throughout the exercises has become a habit and that you check your inner barometer automatically. This can move you forward into becoming even more flexible in your self-talk and more masterful in letting go of what is not working in your life. You can continue to develop these little moments of self-awareness and notice when you make the shift from something negative that was unconscious to something positive that you can move into your life. Trying some new behavior, using your imagination and going outside your usual parameters, visualizing a magic solution, taking an intuitive risk, knowing what you need and asking for it—all of these can become easier with daily practice. Nothing is written in cement. You can scramble it up and create something new.

Let yourself get comfortable and set the timer for twenty minutes. Check your inner barometer for your comfort level with yourself and with your partner. Take a deep breath and hold it for the count of five, and when you exhale, just let go and float into your safe space, and really enjoy being there.

Then let your mind go back to the time when you first started reading this book, the first exercise that you did. Let your mind wander from whatever happened or did not happen from one exercise to another, from one week to another. Perhaps you had a thought, an association, a new feeling, an "ah-ha." Perhaps you had some difficult moments, even painful and sad ones. Perhaps you got in touch with anger that you did not know you had. Just notice. Perhaps you saw something in your partner you had never seen before. Perhaps you were able to say things that you never thought you could say. Perhaps you see something new at this very moment. Just notice and let your mind go wherever it wants to go. And if your mind goes blank that is also part of the process and is just fine.

▶ Tool Kit

As you go through the week notice when you check your inner barometer automatically; notice any time you shift from negative to positive and notice changes in your behavior. Give yourself a message of appreciation for staying with this work.

▶ EXERCISE 34 ◀
THE FLOW OF YOUR LIFE TOGETHER

(I learned this particular exercise from Dr. Peter Nemetschek with whom I co-led a workshop in Rottweil, Germany.)

Go to your special place and bring with you your journal, a pen, the timer, the colored index cards, Post-its, and two different-colored balls of yarn.

Let yourself get settled in your special place and check your inner barometer for your comfort level with yourself and with your partner. Then look up at a spot on the ceiling, take a deep breath, hold it for the count of five, and when you let it go, feel yourself relax. Go to your safe place and enjoy what it looks like, smells like, tastes like, sounds like. When you are ready, let yourself go back to the moment you first met your partner and then when you decided to go on your life's adventure together. You may want to imagine the two of you riding in a boat along the river of life, being carried by the current from one stage of your marriage to another. There may be rocks, rapids, detours, shallow areas, storms, calm, and times when you were not sure where your boat was going and if you could manage the current.

You may have had to ford a great river together and seek shelter from many storms. Or you may see the two of you moving along a road that goes up mountains, down into valleys, through jungles and deserts. You may imagine sitting in your car together going along this road in a terrible thunderstorm that is so powerful it is hard to see a clearing through the windowpane as the wipers move back and forth.

Let your unconscious go wherever it wants to go, and then when you are ready, come back to the room. You may want to take a few moments to write down whatever comes to mind. If you wish, share with your partner for a few minutes.

If you are doing this exercise by yourself, let your mind go back to the beginning of your journey, wherever you want it to be. Picture a road that will take you where you want to go, and notice as you travel along it whether you stay on it, take side trips or detours, or are stopped by obstacles of one sort or another. Just notice. When you have finished, write down whatever comes to mind.

Then each partner picks up one ball of colored yarn. Lay the yarn side by side to represent the day you met. Together move the balls of yarn along the floor. The yarn represents your journey together. Do this right up to the present moment. Every time there is a special event that affects you (the birth of a baby, the loss of a job, the death of a parent) write it down on a Post-it and lay it across the path of the two strings. Did these events help you to get closer or did they separate you? Let the strings move closer together or farther apart in reaction to what happened to you both. Notice what you are feeling as you move the yarn along and talk about the transitions of your life together.

If you are doing this alone, use one color of yarn to represent your core self and the trajectory you wanted your life to take. Use the other colored yarn to represent the journey you have taken, noting with the Post-its the transition points. Did this course veer away from the direction you wanted? If so, how did you get back on course? If you are still not on course, just notice that.

When you are ready, close your eyes and go back to your safe place in your inner mind and just be with yourself for a while, not necessarily having to think anything or do anything. Just enjoy being with the moment. Take as long as you need in the time that you have. Then open your eyes, write down whatever you wish, and share with your partner whatever you wish.

Check your inner barometer for your comfort level with yourself and with your partner.

▶ Tool Kit

During the week, notice any thoughts you have about the line of your life together. Notice if anything comes up that you hadn't thought about. Notice how you feel as you think about it. Make an appointment with your partner to meet in one week to complete the final exercise in this book. Think of a special gift to give your partner at your next meeting to mark the completion of this book. Make it simple—a flower, a shell, a poem, a joke. Actually, it is not a completion, but the beginning of the rest of your life. So it marks the end and the beginning and a transition.

> ▶ **EXERCISE 35** ◀
> MOVING FROM THE PAST
> INTO THE FUTURE:
> FROM FALLING IN LOVE
> TO GROWING IN LOVE

Let yourself get comfortable in your special place and give yourself and your partner a message of appreciation for the work you have done together to get to this last exercise. I hope you have stirred things up in the front and back of your mind and perhaps have felt yourself open up to new and fresh experiences of yourself and of those around you.

Set the timer for twenty minutes and check your inner barometer for your comfort level with yourself and with your partner. Take a deep breath and hold it for the count of five, and when you exhale, just let go and float into your safe space and enjoy being there.

Let your mind review whatever it wants about what you have learned. Notice anything that is new or different. Just be with yourself in whatever way you want for this time.

When the timer rings, open your eyes, write down whatever you would like. Check your inner barometer for your comfort level with yourself and with your partner, and then share with your partner whatever you would like to share.

Set a date for a month from now—you may want to use the first of every month so you can remember—to get together in your special place and review what has been happening. You may want to lay out the yarn for the last month, you may want to redo an exercise, or you may just want to talk. If a disagreement comes up, I suggest you follow the structure in chapter six, exercise fourteen (page 122) "Working with the Iceberg with Your Partner" or exercise fifteen (page 125) "Working with the Iceberg with Your Partner—a Variation." Another way to practice is in chapter nine, exercise twenty-eight (page 164) "Using What You Have Learned to Resolve Disputes About Money." In these situations your usual patterned structure of arguing is interrupted so that you are freed to find new roads to resolution. I encourage you to use these exercises. I know it is easier to slip back into the old ways, the old language. The real work is in making the extra effort to break through into new structures, new language. Every time you do, it gets easier. You have been programmed for a long time. Change won't happen overnight, but with practice and commitment it will happen.

Have fun with this commitment and play with this work. Laugh at how you goofed up your relationship. Learn each time you go backward to shift, turn, and go forward again. Good luck and trust your own natural selves.

Your life together is an adventure. Enjoy it!

I AM DETERMINED

One regret, dear world,
That I am determined not to have
When I am lying on my deathbed
Is that
I did not kiss you enough.

I Heard God Laughing
Renderings of Hafiz (1320–1389)
By Daniel Ladinsky
Copyright 1996

Appendix

This book is about hypnosis and the use of hypnosis for therapeutic and medical purposes. After reading the book, should you decide that you want to use the services of a hypnosis clinician, I encourage you to make sure that whomever you select has a master's-level degree or above in clinical psychotherapy and is state-certified in the profession he/she practices. There are talented people who do not have a clinical degree, but it is not always easy to differentiate them from people who are really not qualified to practice therapeutic hypnosis.

There are only three professionally recognized membership organizations in the United States:

- The American Society of Clinical Hypnosis
- The Society for Experimental and Clinical Hypnosis
- The International Society of Hypnosis

These organizations are acknowledged by professionals who practice hypnosis as the highest and only qualified organizations to recognize people in the field who fulfill required training hours. They each sponsor annual conferences, do trainings, sponsor and support research, and publish journals. Should you wish to find a hypnosis clinician to work with you, the addresses and telephone numbers are listed below.

The American Board of Clinical Hypnosis and its subspecialty boards certify all professionals in medicine, psychiatry, psychology, dentistry, and clinical social work. It is the highest and only reputable organization that certifies for competency by examination. You can be assured that if someone is a diplomate of one of the American Boards of Clinical Hypnosis, he or she has been acknowledged by their peers as most qualified to work with you and that he or she follows the highest ethical standards.

Referral Organizations

American Board of Medical Hypnosis
Donald F. Lynch, Jr., M.D., President
Eastern Virginia School of Medicine
Devine-Tidewater Urology, Ltd.
6333 Center Drive, Building 16
Norfolk, VA 23502
Tel: 757-457-5160
Fax: 757-627-3211

American Board of Psychological Hypnosis
Samuel Migdole, Ed.D., President
23 Broadway
Beverly, MA 01915
Tel: 978-922-2280
Email: Migdole@comcast.com

The American Society of Clinical Hypnosis
140 N. Bloomingdale Road
Bloomingdale, IL 60108-1017
Tel: 630-980-4740
Fax: 630-351-8490
Email: info@asch.net
www.asch.net
You can find out about component sections throughout the country.

International Society of Hypnosis
Austin & Repatriation Medical Centre
Repatriation Campus, 300 Waterdale Road
Heidelberg Heights, VIC 3081
Australia
Tel: + 61 3 9496 4105
Fax: + 61 3 9496 4107
Email: ish-centraloffice@medicine.unimelb.edu.au

Society for Clinical and Experimental Hypnosis
221 Rivermoor Street
Boston, MA 02132
Tel: 617-469-1981
Fax: 617-469-1889
Email: sceh@mspp.edu

Other Organizations

American Hypnosis Board for Clinical Social Work
George Glaser, MSW, DAHB, President
510 S. Congress, Suite 207
Austin, TX 78704
Tel: 512-476-7700
Fax: 512-472-4271
Email: george@georgeglaser.com

American Psychological Association
Division 30—Society for Psychological Hypnosis
750 First Street, N.E.
Washington, DC 20002-4242
Tel: 1-800-374-2721
www.apa.org

Avanta The Virginia Satir Network
2104 S.W. 152nd Street, Suite #2
Burien, WA 98166

Tel: 206-241-7566
Fax: 206-241-7527
Email: office@avanta.net

The Milton H. Erickson Foundation, Inc.
Jeffrey K. Zeig, Ph.D., Director
3606 N. 24th Street
Phoenix, AZ 85016-6500
Tel: 602-956-6196
Fax: 602-956-0519
Email: office@erickson-foundation.org
www.erickson-foundation.org

The Feldenkrais Guild
3611 S.W. Hood Avenue, Suite 100
Portland, OR 97239
Tel: 1-800-775-2118 or 503-221-6612
Fax: 503-221-6616
Email: guild@feldenkrais.com

International Human Learning Resources Network (IHLRN) Satir
Abel Hewitt, President
9330 51st Avenue S.
Seattle, WA 98118-5311
Tel: 206-725-2066
Fax: 206-723-5571
Email: abelhewitt@IHLRN.org

Parsons-Fein Training Institute, Boston
Lawrence Bealey, M.D., Co-Director
Carol Murphy, MSW, LCSW, Co-Director
738 Main Street
Hingham, MA 02043-3386

Parsons-Fein Training Institute, San Francisco
Nick Parsons, LMFT, Director
999 Sutter Street
San Francisco, CA 94109
415-668-9221
Email: nparsons@earthlink.net

Parsons-Fein Training Institute of Sweden
Sven Lindahl, M.A., Licensed Psychotherapist
Persikogatan 74
16563 Hasselby Sweden

For information regarding weekend workshops for couples and for individuals, *Loving in the Here and Now* presentations, audiotapes, videotapes, family reconstruction groups, and other pertinent material, please go to www.lovinginthehereandnow.org.

The Parsons-Fein Training Institute for Psychotherapy and Hypnosis in its 100-hour ASCH-certified Training, has trained certified professional therapists to conduct these groups, workshops, and presentations. (www.pfti.org)